COMPASSION TRANSFORMS CONTEMPT:

A Black Dialogue Expert's Advice for White Progressives on Down-Revving Anger, Creating Connections... and Maybe Changing the World

By David W. Campt PhD
@thedialogueguy
www.thedialoguecompany.com

I AM Publications

Compassion Transforms Conflict: A Black Dialogue Expert's Advice For White Progressives On Down-Revving Anger, Creating Connections...And Maybe Changing The World

Copyright © 2020 by David W. Campt

I AM Publications
(617) 564-1060
contact@iampubs.com
www.iampubs.com

ISBN: 978-1-943382-07-1
First Edition, 2020

DEDICATION

To Geraldine Wiley Campt, 1929 - 2019

Thanks mom for teaching me always to look for the points of connection, because doing so creates more peace...and just feels better.

TABLE OF CONTENTS

CHAPTER 1 — INTRODUCTION   1

A Letter to My Fellow Patriotic Americans Who Are Conservative   13

CHAPTER 2 — CONTEMPT:

IRONIES, HYPOCRISIES, AND TOOLS TO RELEASE YOURSELF   15

CHAPTER 3 — THE REACH METHOD:

A BEST PRACTICE FOR CONNECTING AND PERSUADING   29

CHAPTER 4 — REFLECT:

GETTING READY TO BE EFFECTIVE   37

CHAPTER 5 — ENQUIRE:

MOVING ATTENTION TO WHAT'S BENEATH THE BELIEF   45

CHAPTER 6 — AGREE:

BUILDING RAPPORT AND TRUST THROUGH HIDDEN ALIGNMENT   55

CHAPTER 7 — COAX AND HONOR:

INVITING OTHERS TO SEE EVERYONE CAN BE RIGHT   71

CHAPTER 8 — CONCLUSION:

MOBILIZING COMPASSIONATE DIALOGUE IN OUR HYPER-DIVIDED TIME   83

APPENDIX 1 — RESOURCES ON EMPATHY BASED ENGAGEMENT   89

APPENDIX 2 — A TOOL TO IMPROVE CONVERSATIONS ABOUT PRESIDENT TRUMP   90

APPENDIX 3 — CONSERVATIVE VERSUS LIBERAL LIFESTYLE ASSESSMENT   92

APPENDIX 4 — AGENDA TEMPLATE FOR GROUP MEETINGS   94

PREFACE

Welcome to my seventh book about the process of interpersonal dialogue. I have written this handbook with the greatest sense of urgency.

My intense interest in dialogue arose within my family, mostly observing the relationship between my parents, married 66 years until my mom died in 2019. Their abiding love inspired me, but their frequent intense bickering upset me; the combination sparked my interest in the necessity of healing human dialogue.

In 1960-1970s Detroit, the pervasive public racial conflict reinforced my interest in developing practical methods to improve how people talk to each other. I observed the inability of leaders of the entrenched white power structure and the ascendant black population to engage in civil conversation. These two experiences fostered my passion for strengthening dialogue methods generally, and for discussions about racism specifically.

This dialogue handbook does not provide direct guidance on how to talk about racism. My experiences with racism are not shocking to those familiar with it: landlords slamming doors shut at apartments I had been invited to rent, inappropriate questions challenging my qualifications for prestigious positions I attained, being handcuffed by police after explaining I was the victim of an assault, and multiple instances of hearing the drive-by verbal assaults of "nigger."

The overlap between my interest in racism as a defining experience of American life and in dialogue as the solution to problems has propelled me toward the life of racial dialogue facilitation. I have worked to harness the power of dialogue for various clients, including President Clinton, Congressman John Lewis and his congressional peers, and Kareem Abdul Jabbar to increase understanding between Native Americans, black Buffalo Soldier re-enactors and white descendants of settlers.

The focus of my dialogue work shifted with the Presidential election of 2016.

I could not process the election result as anything but a massive failure by white allies. The election result proved that, as a group, white progressives were stunningly incapable of conversing with centrist- and conservative-leaning white people about an important but simple question: Was candidate Donald Trump too racially problematic to support?

The disastrous election results showed that white progressives were ignorant of the fact that successfully persuading people with different worldviews happens neither from avoiding conversations about differences of opinion nor from blasting them with sanctimonious soliloquies. My attention shifted to enhancing white progressives' abilities to create productive and persuasive exchanges with other whites. My goal became identifying and refining best practice dialogue methods white allies could adopt and spread as a positive contagion.

After having authored four books and having guided thousands of aspiring white allies in pursuit of my goal, as 2020 began, I asked myself: what do I need to do so that I know I did my best to support the success of white allies, and therefore racial progress?

I realized that I needed to increase my focus on the underlying issue of compassion (a persuasion best practice), considering that white people are remarkably contemptuous of people they label as "different." I also saw it was necessary to confront white progressives' incapacity to engage conservatives in effective conversations about politics.

White progressives are particularly apprehensive about conversations across the political divide. A 2017 Pew study found that white liberals are much more likely to define a conversation across the Pro-Trump/Anti-Trump divide as "stressful and frustrating" than white conservatives, Latino progressives, and black progressives.

This handbook addresses a glaring deficiency among white progressives which could help Trump win reelection; a calamity for all, particularly for people of color, and for American democracy. The most direct path for a white progressive to change a conservative's vote might not involve a conversation on race.

During the Civil Rights movement, black folks in America divined successful ways to stay resolute, compassionate, and disciplined in transforming racist attitudes among those who characterized them as cultural enemies. I believe that white progressives can learn from these ways and do the same.

I offer this handbook as a workable plan for white progressives to effectively converse with white conservatives. My intention is for them to get busy compassionately engaging, to help our nation move past this catastrophic president and transform America with the racial healing and other vital cultural rebuilding work that has been long overdue.

CHAPTER 1

INTRODUCTION

Chapter 1 — Introduction

SECTION 1: INTENTION OF THIS BOOK

Throughout the United States, both progressives and conservatives are lamenting the level of division in our culture and in our politics. Polling data tells us that 81% of Americans are worried by the level of division in the country.[1] Essentially, the one thing that unites Americans is their concern about how divided they are.

> This handbook is for politically progressive people who want go beyond worrying and actually do something about this divisiveness by changing how they interact with conservatives.

While both progressives and conservatives lament the divisiveness in the country, both are deathly worried about the 2020 election. Many think of the election as pivotal for the future of the country, and especially for "their" side. Progressives, the primary target of this handbook, fear that the reelection of President Trump will set back the progressive movement and the country for decades, given the administration's rollback on climate change and the environment, the social safety net, the judiciary system, civil rights enforcement, and a host of other issues. Conservatives have their own set of ideas about the abyss the nation will fall into unless President Trump is re-elected.

Naturally, each side blames the other's recalcitrance for the divisiveness they lament.

The question that we should be thinking about is: what can everyday Americans do about the polarization that we claim to care so much about?

In recent years, there has been an increased array of books aimed at raising awareness about divisiveness. Many esteemed thinkers have tried to shake people by their heads and shoulders about it. Arthur Brooks, Erica Etelson, and Gleb Tsipursky[2] are among those who have written excellent and inspiring books about the divides in Americans and have provided important insights that could fuel a national project of knitting our political culture back together.

---

1   Partisan Antipathy: More Intense, More Personal, Pew Research Center (October 10, 2019), www.pewresearch.com

2   Brooks, Arthur (2019) Love Your Enemies: How Decent People Can Save America from the Culture of Contempt, New York, Broadside Books.

   Etelson, Erica (2020) Beyond Contempt: How Liberals Can Communicate Across the Great Divide, Gabriola Island, British Columbia, New Society Publishers.

   Tsipursky, Gleb (expected April 2020) The Blindspots Between Us: How to Overcome Unconscious Cognitive Bias and Build Better Relationships, Oakland, CA, New Harbinger Publications.

Compassion Transforms Conflic

Chapter 1 — Introduction

I have been asked to endorse a few of these books (Etelson and Tsipursky), and have done so enthusiastically. These books about polarization and divides—and many others I have not read—should be required reading in modern high school civics classes and for every adult book group in the country. If the historians who say that we are more divided than we have been since the Civil War are correct, we are in the midst of a significant national crisis. Our country's civic culture—which is essential to a functioning democracy—is at risk. Given the polling on the topic, these fine books focused on polarization should be non-fiction best-sellers.

These books are great for getting Americans motivated about the polarization problem. They are also great for inspiring us to think about what is possible; the texts include numerous stories about what happens when people have changed their behavior, engaged people who see the world very differently, and often created transformation in themselves, their relationships, and their communities. We need these stories that remind us of the magic Americans can make if we are going to do the hard work of revisiting our reactions to folks on the other side of the divide.

This handbook is highly aligned with these admittedly greater works; it will focus on some key issues that they explore to different extents, but for the most part do not drill down on. This handbook focuses specifically on what exactly people should do during interactions with people on the other side. This handbook also points you toward a path to developing the ability to behave differently so that you can get different results.

My assumption in writing this handbook is that, for the most part, you are not looking for motivation about why progressives need to change their behavior toward conservatives. These bigger books do that quite well. My presumption is that you are already somewhat or highly motivated, and that you have acquired this handbook because you want your interactions with conservatives to be less laced with unpleasant tension, or because you want to become more persuasive when you talk to conservatives.

If you are motivated by both the peace-building and influence-wielding motivations, that is just fine. We are fortunate to live in a universe where the best practices for reducing tension and for increasing influence are the same.

Because of my assumption that you are already motivated, this handbook spends a minority of its pages on why progressives should change their behavior; the majority of pages will be on what progressives should do and how they should train themselves to interact differently. This handbook focuses on this question: *What exactly do progressives need to do so that their conversations with someone on the opposite side of the ideological divide builds connections and increases their influence?*

It is on this issue of action that this handbook is overwhelmingly focused. This handbook addresses questions such as:

- What are best practices when trying to influence someone in one-on-one conversation?

- Is there a way of understanding the differences between conservatives and liberals that tends to lead to less contempt between the two camps?

- What is the internal work that we need to do to change our attitude about people on the other side of the political divide?

- What are specific exercises available to be prepared to have a different kind of conversation?

- When folks finds themselves reverting to old habits of ineffective arguing, what are some things that get the conversation back on track?

- How can a progressive help a conservative relax and become more trusting?

- If differences of opinion start to emerge, what can be done in the conversation to help reestablish a sense of connection?

- What are the best ways to move a conservative toward a more progressive point of view?

WHO IS THIS BOOK FOR?

My entire career has been dedicated to spreading principles and practices of dialogue. I deeply believe that dialogue is one of the most important things human beings can do to create a better world. It is particularly important in democracies. People everywhere need better conversations across all divides: race, gender, sexual orientation, disability status, and on and on.

I believe that more and better dialogue can help solve almost any human problem, and I think every human being should be trained in core dialogue skills. Nevertheless, this handbook is not aimed at everyone concerned about the divide between liberals and conservatives. This book is aimed specifically at people who might be called progressive or liberal.

> The potential of white progressives inspires me deeply, and the behavior of actual white progressives both amuses and aggravates me. Some of my ideas need to be said and heard in specifically racial terms, even though this handbook is not focused on talking about race.

More pointedly, the target audience for this book is white progressives. For reasons that will be discussed, I think that white progressives have a special opportunity to reach conservatives that needs to be highlighted. Further, I have a great deal of experience coaching white progressives about how to grapple with their internal challenges in dealing with conservatives. In addition, there are some lessons I have learned from living as a black man that white liberals need to know, and that are best expressed in an explicitly cross-cultural and multiracial context.

The best practices for creating peaceful encounters across the divide and for maximizing one's influence are general and can be used by people of any ideological stripe. After the general principles are explained, this handbook will explore in depth how these universal ideas can be used by progressives trying to connect with and persuade conservatives.

If you are someone who leans right, my hope is that you will not be offended by this focus on people who lean left. If you are a conservative person you might find this book helpful, since the book builds upon universal principles—but you will have to do additional mental work. Feel free to partake in the mental labor necessary to translate the ideas here into methods you can use to connect with and persuade liberals.

If you are a conservative who wants to do something about the way that our current ways of relating across the divide put our democracy at risk, you are I are allies. If you are wondering why someone supposedly committed to cross-ideological dialogue would address only one side, please read the letter to my conservative brothers and sisters that appears at the end of this chapter.

HOW THIS HANDBOOK IS STRUCTURED

The ideas in the rest of this introductory chapter focus on:
- The outline of this handbook
- Ways this handbook can be used
- Reasons that people with various motivations should form practice groups around this material

Chapter 2 provides contextual factors for the work that progressives should be engaged in. The chapter includes some national context that every American should understand about the modern polarization problem, as well as hypocrisies between the nature of progressive ideology and the typically awful behavior progressives exhibit toward conservatives. In addition, it will explore the science relevant to creating more productive encounters. Chapter 2 also includes findings about the nature of progressives and conservatives that many people have found eye-opening in my workshops.

The rest of the book focuses on what you should do to use all of that contextual information to change how you communicate. Chapter 3 introduces the conversational strategy that embodies a (perhaps *the*) best practice in communication across the ideological aisle. I call this approach the REACH method (Reflect, Enquire, Agree, Coax, Honor). Other experts have their own names for what is largely the same method for sequencing a conversation to maximize rapport and influence. Chapters 4-7 review the major steps of the REACH method.

Chapter 4 – Reflect – This chapter focuses on how you can center yourself at the start of an encounter, as well as actions you can take so that you can keep making good choices as the interaction unfolds.

Chapter 5 – Enquire – This chapter focuses on different ways to ask questions to get your conversation partners talking about what lies beneath their conservative beliefs. Having a conversational focus on what is underneath a belief is a best-practice way of building rapport.

Chapter 6 – Agree – This chapter focuses on ways you can create a sense of alignment or even agreement to further build on the rapport you have already begun to establish.

Chapter 7 – Coax and Honor – This chapter focuses on the part of the conversation where you try to actually influence someone by inviting them to come to your point of view (Coax). Your goal is to try to end the conversation so that they do not have the feeling that they have been told they were wrong, but instead feel like they have been invited build to on what they know and add an additional insight (Honor).

Chapter 8 – Conclusion – This chapter provides concluding thoughts to keep in mind as you try to take on the task of training yourself away from your current communication patterns and toward ones that have the best chance of being more effective.

WAYS TO USE THIS BOOK

This handbook aims to nudge progressives toward being forces for better discourse around America's challenges and its future. There are a number of ways you can use this book toward this end. I will present them in increasing order of effectiveness:

AS A WAY TO SPARK CONVERSATION WITH A CONSERVATIVE

Part of the reason this handbook has a provocative title and cover is so it can be used as a conversation starter, particularly with a conservative. Don't be embarrassed or anxious to leave this book where your conservative family member or friend might see it. Even if they might be irritated that this handbook focuses on strategies destined to reach and persuade conservative people, there are no secret tricks here. **Americans need to be talking to each other about how they talk to each other.**

If this handbook prompts you and your conservative cousin to have some conversation about ways that you should talk to each other that will feel better, this book is doing its job. If conservative people are even remotely curious about this handbook, direct their attention to the letter to conservative people at the end of this chapter.

AS A WAY TO SPARK CONVERSATION WITH OTHER PROGRESSIVES

It is my belief that not only do progressives not understand how to talk to conservatives in a way that uses best practices, but they also rarely have useful conversations amongst themselves about what might be more or less effective methods of conversation.

From doing my workshops with thousands of progressives over the past few years, it is clear to me that when the idea of talking to conservatives and/or Trump supporters comes up, most people do not go much past complaining about their frustrations in such conversations. Generally, when I press people on the lessons they have learned from attempts at conversation, they usually give up. "You can't talk to those people." Or they make statements like, "I just get too frustrated...and those people are crazy anyway."

Unfortunately, what people do not do is talk about what methods work best. It is useful to have a conversation with another progressive about the following question: From your own experience or what you have read, what are the ways of talking to conservatives and Trump supporters that have the best chances of success?

Even if you only leave this handbook where other progressives might see it and you create such a conversation, this handbook is still doing part of its job.

AS A TEXT TO READ FROM START TO FINISH AND PUT ON THE SHELF

You might read this handbook in the way that many read other books—from start to finish, then remember key things learned, and apply them as needed. There are benefits to be had from doing this. For instance, there are a number of ideas in Chapter 2 about the context of modern polarization that you might both enlightening and motivating. In addition, there is a good chance that you will remember the principles and steps of the REACH method. If you read the book all the way through and just put it down, you will not learn as much as you might if you engage the iterative process of reading it, trying the methods, reflecting on them, and moving on the other methods. But, given the terrible state of discourse in the country, just exposing yourself to ideas about how you might communicate differently is good in and of itself.

READ A CHAPTER, PRACTICE, REFLECT, READ ANOTHER CHAPTER, REPEAT

This handbook explains the REACH method of managing conversation in a step-by-step fashion in successive chapters. My hope is that you read the book all the way through, then actively engage it starting with the Reflect chapter. Ideally, on your second pass you will read a chapter, take time to practice the methods of that chapter, make observations about what you learned, and then proceed to the other chapters and do the same process. At the end of each chapter on the REACH steps there are questions to think about before you engage the processes of that chapter. Each chapter also includes self-reflection questions to think about after you practice the step in the wild with actual people.

The handbook is structured this way out of a recognition that moving to best practices in communication is difficult, and for most people it requires a substantial breaking of habits and adaption of new behaviors. Some people can take on a number of new steps all at once, but most people trying to learn a new set of skills do better by taking them on one at a time.

As an additional tool for helping you learn the methods, most chapters will provide guidelines about how you might engage the methods at different levels of difficulty.

And the best way to use this book is…

USE THIS BOOK AS THE BASIS OF A PROGRESSIVE PRACTICE GROUP

Most people will make much better progress on changing the way they relate to conservatives if they are part of a group of 2-10 people who meet regularly (in person or online) to discuss their attempts to communicate differently. Almost certainly, if you actually try to engage the REACH methods, you will experience a range of outcomes. There will be: times when you plan to use them and fail to engage when an appropriate moment comes; times when you execute them and get less apparent impact than you hope; and times when you execute the methods and have great success. When you are in the up-and-down path of developing a new habit, it will be helpful for you have the reinforcement of a group of people with whom you can share your trials and triumphs.

To support using a group to boost your engagement of the REACH method, each chapter on its major steps will include group discussion questions. These will typically build on the individual reflection questions provided.

Reasons for Creating a Practice Group

I know that being a part of a group trying to learn something can be a headache. Here is why you should consider it: American culture is primarily argumentative and not oriented to listening. Thus, adapting the communications strategies laid out here will require a significant shift for most people.

The REACH method of managing a conversation will encourage you to take a moment to collect yourself before engaging; this itself is counter-cultural, given the way that modern American culture places so much attention on each person reflexively conveying their own perspective when in conflict. Pausing to first explore someone else's opinion is countercultural. Prioritizing agreement at a time when people value raw self-expression as most authentic—especially at first—is countercultural. Finally, trying to find the synthesis between different points of view is seen by many as weak instead of strong.

The methods of relating to conservatives taught in this handbook are, regrettably, countercultural to current American practices. While some people can change their habits by themselves, most do better with encouragement and support from others doing the same thing.

Thus, by taking on the task of retraining of yourself, you are swimming against the current of the cultural stream. You are more likely to maintain the energy needed to do so if you are connected to other people doing the same thing. You may get discouraged. The methods of communication described here are virtually guaranteed to make talking to conservatives more harmonious, but I can not guarantee that you will change their point of view. These methods only offer you the best *chance* to change their minds. Conversions are not guaranteed. We will discuss the attitude that is most suggested about changing people's minds in light of this, but it is useful to know that there will be many times when you will use these methods and still NOT move a conservative's opinions. A value of staying connected to a group of others working these methods is that your spirit for compassion-based methods can be buoyed by others' successes, even when you personally don't have a success to report.

WHAT MIGHT BE THE ORGANIZING PRINCIPLE OF A PRACTICE GROUP?
A Strategy to Influence Elections

The methods discussed in this handbook are the best way to win over persuadable conservatives. Thus, it would make sense to form a practice group as part of an electoral strategy in a voting area where progressives and conservatives are in a tight battle. At the national level, President Trump won the electoral college by a margin of 78,000 votes in Wisconsin, Michigan, and Pennsylvania, which is less than 1% of the vote in those states. Imagine if in those states only one out of twenty (5%) progressive voters engaged in best-practice persuasion strategies with conservatives in their circle of contacts, and only one in three of those turned a vote. This would move about 1.6% of the votes, changing the election outcome. It would make sense for progressives in cities, counties, or states with sharply divided voting patterns to start practice groups to grow the movement for more effective engagement of people in our circles of influence. The central organizing question of such a group might be: How can progressives (in our district, city, county, or states) influence persuadable conservative friends and neighbors before the next election?

Doing Your Part to Combat Polarization

Over 80% of Americans are concerned about political divisiveness, but most think that the core problem is people on the other side of the divide. If you know or could find other people who want to actually do something about this, putting a few hours a month into a practice group is a way to actively fight against polarization. This strategy might be particularly relevant if you are joining forces with other progressives who are part of a community or organization where those divisions are evident. There are civic organizations (such as Rotary clubs), churches, and other non-political groups that are divided ideologically where political tensions come out explicitly or where people completely avoid talking about politics because they fear these tensions. Both excessive confrontation and total avoidance of politics weaken our civic life and the health of our communities. You and other progressives can potentially improve the culture of your community by becoming people who demonstrate that conversations across ideological lines can be mutually respectful. The central organizing question of such a group might be: How can progressive [Rotarians, Masons, Lions Club members, etc.] help make our culture more accommodating of healthy political discussion?

A Spiritual Group Based on Expanding Compassion

As was/will be discussed, engaging in the steps of the REACH method means putting aside how much you might detest the views of your conservative conversation partner and making a decision to treat them with respect and compassion. As such, using the steps of this method is a spiritual practice. Accordingly, some will convene around the motivation of increasing their demonstrated compassion in a world where compassion is lacking. Some groups centered on these methods as tools for compassion might be organized around specific religious or spiritual traditions. The central organizing question of such a group might be: How can progressive [Jews/Lutherans/Baha'is etc.] spread compassion in these divided times?

A POINT OF TERMINOLOGY

Progressives often spend a lot of energy highlighting what might be considered relatively minor disagreements that they have with each other. For instance, I have met people who take umbrage at being called a liberal and insist that they be called "progressive." While this distinction might be meaningful in some academic discussions, my usual inner reaction when people get overly excited about such distinctions is "Ain't that cute?"

In this handbook, left-leaning, liberal, and progressive all mean the same thing. Similarly, right-leaning, conservative, and Trump supporters also mean the same thing, unless otherwise stated.

ROLE OF RACE IN THIS HANDBOOK

This book is explicitly not about how white progressives should talk to white conservatives about things related to race and racism; I have written or co-written four other books about that topic. (You can find them at whiteallytoolkit.com and at thedialoguecompany.com). It is also not about how white progressives should talk to non-white people. This handbook is about how white progressives should talk to white conservatives about political issues that are not related to race.

Conversations about race have their own opportunities, risks, and dynamics that merit separate discussion and guidance. Even though this book is not about those factors, my experience in coaching white progressives on their communication patterns has taught me a great deal about the social and psychological dynamics affecting and afflicting contemporary white people, and these lessons—plus the urgency of the 2020 election—have led to this handbook.

In addition, this handbook's guidance about how white progressives can be more effective peace-builders and influencers reflect my twenty-five years as a dialogue practitioner. I would expect that similarly experienced white peers might offer comparable ideas about communications best practices if they were to address this topic. However, this handbook will include a few comments that my fellow white peers would not make. Some of my observations about the challenges for white progressives reflect that people of color have had to develop habits, tools, and wisdom for dealing with problematic white people.

From time to time, I will offer ideas about the challenges at hand as reflections from a my specifically black perspective. To delineate these ideas, I will present them as coming from an alter ego.

This alter ego is a longtime observer of the ways of white folks; his experience of them is as varied as white people are. He finds their racial cluelessness tiring, their earnestness inspiring, and their self-righteousness annoying, to name three illustrations. When reflecting on white progressives, he often finds himself thinking "Bless their heart," the same way southern people do. People often employ this linguistic trick when they find themselves lapsing into a jaundiced view of someone but want to remind themselves not to forget the inherent goodness that lies beneath their behavior, no matter what they are doing at that moment.

Because it makes me laugh, I am going to give this alter ego the 70s-esque nickname BrothaMan.

A Letter to My Fellow Patriotic Americans Who Are Conservative

Thank you for reading this letter that lies within a handbook designed for liberals. Your decision to pay any attention to this document is truly an act of generosity and grace on your part, since not only is this handbook not addressed to you, it is aimed specifically at those who want to change the minds of people like you.

Certainly, part of the reason I wrote this handbook is to pursue a goal you almost certainly oppose, which is creating a successful progressive movement. But the bigger motivation for writing the book is a goal that you and other conservatives do support, which is building a stronger America. I deeply believe that American democracy is in serious decline. Over the past few decades, liberals and conservatives have grown to see each other decreasingly as opponents they respect and increasingly as enemies they despise. This is not the vision of the country handed down to us by Madison, Jefferson, and Lincoln, nor the vision bequeathed to us by Frederick Douglas, Harriet Tubman, or Martin Luther King, Jr.

All of these American heroes envisioned a nation where people who had deep political disagreements could have a drink together without angry verbal warfare if current events came up. They did not imagine that having Thanksgiving dinner without rage and tears would mean having negotiated pre-agreements to not talk about the challenges facing the nation.

There has been an erosion of the shared sense that Americans can find common purpose and values even in the midst of heated disagreements. We need conservative and liberal Americans working side-by-side on the problem of our degraded discourse. We also need them to be working separately on this problem, and trying to make sure their own group is not making things worse. I hope this handbook helps liberals do some of the work that is theirs to do.

From the attitudes and behavior I have seen among white progressives, I expect that you might have been at least once or twice assailed by completely unwarranted assumptions about your morality, intelligence, generosity, rationality, or other qualities by liberals who were triggered by your very presence. Progressives frequently deny basic dignity to conservatives, and I expect that a progressive has likely done this to you. Even though I did not know those people, I apologize for that. Those progressives are part of the political coalition I am in, so I am a part of the culture that produced those moments. This handbook is my attempt to produce fewer of those moments I regret being connected to.

My apology by proxy should not be interpreted as expressing a view on the question of whether progressives or conservatives are the bigger source of our divisiveness problems. If you, I, and the progressive who owns this handbook were to discuss divisiveness over a drink, I would likely disagree with both of you on the nature of America's polarization problem. Nevertheless, I believe that people should take responsibility for their piece of a problem, whether their piece is the bigger or smaller portion.

This handbook is one attempt to address the problems my fellow progressives are causing which hurt democracy. The coaching in this book highlights best practices in more peaceful communication and persuasion and helps progressives apply them. I think that our nation would be better if conservatives learned them too. If you know a conservative person who wants to bring these peacebuilding methods to folks on the right, feel free to direct them to me. I would love to be of assistance to them or perhaps collaborate with them.

Thanks for reading this letter and I wish you many good conversations with conservatives and liberals about what we all need to do to make our democracy better.

Dr. David Campt

@thedialogueguy

CHAPTER 2

CONTEMPT: IRONIES, HYPOCRISIES, AND TOOLS TO RELEASE YOURSELF

Chapter 2 — Contempt

There are several major ideas that may be useful for you to review before delving into the REACH method. The exercises in the rest of the handbook build on these ideas. Each of these major ideas will be discussed in a separate section.

Section 1 discusses the fact that the contempt many progressives feel for people they politically disagree with (and the contempt they sometimes feel for people in other parts of the progressive coalition) is something that has been purposely stoked by leaders they probably don't admire or respect.

Section 2 discusses the inherent tensions between progressivism and the contempt for conservatives that often drives progressives' behavior in conversations.

Section 3 discusses some important findings and ways of thinking about the similarities and differences between progressives and conservatives. Many progressives have told me that these conceptual tools greatly enhance their ability to let go of the contempt they often feel and display toward conservatives.

SECTION 1: THE CONTEMPT AGENDA

> Putin is playing all of us, and when we indulge in contempt for other Americans, we are doing what he wants.

Any moderately informed student of American history knows that there have been important ideological divisions in the nation since its inception. At the same time, it is important that Americans of all ideological stripes remember that current levels of division are being purposely enhanced through a well-funded attack by Russian President Vladimir Putin.[3]

There is widespread evidence that Russia has spent hundreds of millions of dollars on manipulating both mass and social media in service of exacerbating tensions between disparate American groups. The left/right divide is key to that strategy, as are divisions about race and racism. Putin's goal is to leverage the fact that media exacerbates ideological silos and leads to people demonizing others with different perspectives, making this demonization even worse so that more Americans turn against each other.

Any time you see an ad or social media post that riles you, that makes you disdainful of other progressives with slight ideological differences, or that causes you outrage at the despicable behavior of conservatives, you should remember that you could be being manipulated at that very moment by Putin's agenda. If it turns out that the unbelievably enraging behaviors or statements that make your blood boil come from actual Americans, it is still possible that the person behaving that way has been manipulated by these same malevolent forces.

---

3   Business Insider, (October 17, 2017) 'Our task was to set Americans against their own government': New details emerge about Russia's trolling operation.

This manipulation is a long-run problem that cannot be solved just by verbalizing it. Still, it is important to remember and talk about the fact that our disdain for others is being purposely stoked. Talking about it—to other progressives and also to conservatives—is important. Conversations about this ongoing media attack with our ideological comrades and opponents can help lessen the impact of such manipulation on ourselves and others.

FOSTERING CONTEMPT AS A POLITICAL SUCCESS MODEL

Putin is not the only world leader who sees fostering contempt within America as their primary business model. The same is true of President Trump. As columnist E.J. Dionne says, President Trump's political model is to exercise his base around the disdain that they think is aimed at them from liberals—cast as big city people, the college-educated, LGBT folk, environmentalists, and people of color and the whites who like them. Emphasizing the all-too-real disdain that white liberals frequently express toward white conservatives is a core part of President Trump's organizing strategy and political rhetoric.

By carrying and nurturing their disdain for Trump and his supporters and by thinking and talking about them as moral and emotional miscreants, progressives make it more difficult to positively engage conservatives when they do have occasion to interact with them. Naturally, when conservative feel this disdain, they experience the narrative that Trump has promoted and that drives enthusiasm for him.

All of the above is not to suggest that progressive people should not recognize and oppose President Trump's multiple deleterious effects on American politics and our culture. It is not to suggest that people should not mobilize themselves for action to counter this impact with all the energy they can muster. The challenge is to engage in those mobilizing and organizing projects while maintaining and broadcasting compassion for individual conservatives that they interact with.

SECTION 2: OUR ACTIONS ARE AT ODDS WITH OUR HIGHEST BELIEFS

There are many paradoxes in the modern progressive movement under President Trump. Many liberals see the President as a significant throwback to a host of noxious cultural undercurrents they thought America had long since let go of. To many liberals, he represents the lower demons of our nature, as reflected in racism, xenophobia, patriarchal hegemony, anti-environmentalism, and so on that he espouses in both his rhetoric and policies.

As a result of this perception, many liberals think of both the President and the roughly half of the American public who supports him as malefactors that have merited scorn, disapproval, derision, and loathing. Progressives often say things like, "Hillary was right…they ARE deplorable!" In the same vein, a widely shared meme on the left is "Anyone who supports a racist is a racist."

Given that President Trump is causing the rollback of a great many advances created before him, and that his rise is associated with an increase in hate crimes, corruption, and a general increase in meanness by emboldened conservatives, it is understandable that many liberals think of Trump supporters as enemies. Many spokespeople on the left have written articles about the way that talking to Trump supporters is a waste of energy and that they need to be outvoted, not persuaded, because persuasion is impossible.

Progressives need to acknowledge that though thinking of Trump supporters as enemies of cultural progress is understandable, doing so contradicts basic tenets of the progressive tradition, such as:

1. Every human being is worthy of love.

2. Every person has both good qualities and bad qualities.

3. Redemption is always a possibility that we should keep in mind.

4. Human systems work better when people are in dialogue, as opposed to some people dictating what everyone must do.

5. Hating people is corrosive to the people doing the hating.

> The paradox of deeply opposing the ideas, behaviors, and policies of a huge social movement while not hating the members of that movement is a paradox that white progressives must learn how to embrace.

Under normal conditions, 90% of liberals would agree that these ideas are important parts of what being progressive is about. However, given the polarization in American culture, it is often remarkably difficult for people to apply these ideas to how they feel about Trump supporters, much less Trump himself. I have been in Christian churches and asked people to name positive qualities of President Trump (see appendix 2), and people have hollered out, "He's not like every other human being; he has NO positive qualities!"

I have found that if you keep challenging most white liberals on their deep-seated contempt for Trump and his supporters, they will admit that their perspective is somewhat at odds with the progressive values of shared humanity, empathy, inclusion, redemption, and so on. At first, they usually take refuge in how awful he and his supporters are. But under more questioning, most white liberals, especially ones with a religious or spiritual orientation, know their inability to acknowledge Trump's basic humanity—including the possibility of him having good qualities—is an emotional and spiritual failure on their part.

You don't have to be a person of color or follow spiritual teachings to see the corrosive impact of the deep enmity that liberals have for followers of Trump. Such negative passions undermine democracy. As Robert Kennedy said the day after Martin Luther King was assassinated:

"When you teach a man to hate and fear his brother, when you teach that he is a lesser man because of his color or his beliefs or the policies he pursues, when you teach that those who differ from you threaten your freedom or your job or your family, then you also learn to confront others not as fellow citizens, but as enemies — to be met not with cooperation but with conquest, to be subjugated and mastered."

In order for the nation to move forward, white progressives must find a way to thoroughly oppose what today's conservatives are doing, while still thinking of conservative people as worthy of respect and dignity. One workshop participant shouted "Love the sinner, hate the sin," when reminded of the importance of extending compassion to people that liberals feel are hurting the nation by promoting conservative views.

BROTHAMAN SEZ — TWO-EDGED SWORD

My experience is that while most black progressives—especially ones over 45—don't like Trump supporters and are suspicious of them, it is easier for them to acknowledge his basic humanity. To them, Trump supporters represent an amped-up version of regrettable qualities of whiteness that people have been struggling with for centuries.

Spiritual leaders throughout history—Martin Luther King, Jr, Mahatma Ghandi, Jesus, and many others—have reminded us that the sword of hatred cuts both ways, injuring both the target of the weapon and the one who holds it. People who have had to grapple with centuries of oppression have learned this, but sadly, many white liberals today often seem unable to remember this basic tenet about indulging contempt. Because black people have always had to forge relationships with white people whose contempt for them simmered just below the surface, it generally seems easier for black people to resist the inclination to seeing Trump's supporters as people who should be despised. We have learned over the centuries that nurturing a sizzling antipathy for white people because of their problematic whiteness may be temporarily self-protective, but in the long run it burns us. As a general rule, it seems easier for black people to see Trump supporters as people who need to be politically defeated as opposed to enemies who need to be hated and socially crushed.

> Black folks have had 400 years of practice in being disappointed by white people. What we are seeing now is hard to watch, but is hardly surprising.

AN ADDITIONAL PARADOX FOR PROGRESSIVES

If you want to successfully use the REACH method of influencing people, there is an additional paradox that you need to embrace. This paradox is not about your attitude to your conversation partners, but about the conversation itself. It has to do with how you manage your intention during the conversation.

In order to execute the best practice communications practices that are most likely to lead to changing someone's mind, you must do two things that pull in opposite directions. For starters, it is important to mobilize a deeply felt will within you so that you can adapt a general communication plan to deal with the unexpected variations that conversations have. Every conversation is different, and will have its own sidetracks, rabbit holes, unexpected points of connection and insight, and so on. In order to make good decisions about navigating the conversation well, you must remain deeply committed to your vision of a better connection and perhaps a changed mind so that you can keep yourself focused on the goal.

At the same time, you cannot become overly attached to the outcome of changing the mind of your conversation partner. If you do, most people will sense that you have an agenda of changing them, and this perception will make them less open to the ideas you want to them to entertain.

Put differently, you have to want them to change their minds enough to control your natural reactions and stick to a plan. But…you can't want them to change too badly. If you are too intensely focused on the goal of opinion change, not only will they likely sense this and resist, but also you will probably make poor choices in the conversation, such as rushing it along.

For the method to be most effective, you must be deeply committed to the possibility that the conversation might be transformative, and yet you can't be emotionally attached to being successful. If you are overly attached to the outcome, your emotion itself will make it less likely that you will achieve it.

SECTION 3: CONCEPTUAL TOOLS TO HELP YOU ADJUST YOUR ATTITUDE

Many of the participants in my workshops have expressed that it is easier to lower their contempt reaction to conservatives after learning about some important differences between conservatives and liberals that emerge from the field of social psychology.

This section summarizes some of these key differences. Much of this material comes from a specific subfield called moral foundations theory, which focuses on the ways that people construct their moral outlook. A popular book about this is the New York Times best seller The Righteous Mind, written by Professor Jonathan Haidt.

IDEOLOGICAL DIFFERENCES ARE NOT JUST ABOUT POLITICS; THEY ARE ALSO ABOUT MORALITY

Moral foundations theorists posit that around the world, there are five (some experts include six) ways that people evaluate the morality of a person, a community, or an action.

LIBERALS AND CONSERVATIVES BASE THEIR MORALITY ON DIFFERENT VALUES:

- **Care:** defined as cherishing and protecting others.
  What is the degree to which the action, person, or community is operating in a way that shows sufficient caring?
  Opposite: harm.

- **Fairness:** defined as rendering justice according to shared principles.
  What is the degree to which the action, person, or community is operating in a way that demonstrates the appropriate level of justice and fairness for the relevant parties?
  Opposites: cheating, injustice.

- **Loyalty:** defined as appropriately supporting your group, family, or nation.
  What is the degree to which the action, person, or community demonstrates appropriate prioritization of groups that merit attention and regard?
  Opposites: betrayal, disloyalty.

- **Authority or Respect:** defined as submitting to tradition and legitimate authority.
  What is the degree to which the action, person, or community demonstrates appropriate regard and submission to relevant sources of authority?
  Opposites: subversion, chaos.

- **Sanctity or Purity:** defined as keeping the needed focus for keeping things in their original state.
  What is the degree to which actions, people, or communities sufficiently recognize and oppose the forces that take things away from their original, unmarred, unblemished state?
  Opposite: degradation.

- **Liberty**: defined as fostering freedom from domination.
  What is the degree to which actions or people operate in a way that reduces the likelihood of inappropriate dominance of some entities by others?
  Opposites: domination, oppression, tyranny.

Note: Compared to the first five frameworks, there is less consensus among scholars about whether the Liberty framework is truly foundational.

According to moral foundations theory, most cultures and subcultures base the definition of good or bad behavior on some combination of these differing values. Different cultures value each of these dimensions to varying degrees. Haidt argues that American liberals emphasize the values of caring and fairness and tend to put a low value on loyalty, authority, and sanctity. By contrast, American conservatives tend to put significant emphasis on these dimensions, although they do not completely devalue caring and fairness. Haidt argues that conservatives tend to emphasize all five dimensions. Further, says Haidt, one way that conservatives suss out liberals is by the way that progressives tend not to talk about loyalty, authority, and purity. As we will discuss, you can attempt to leverage this fact in your conversations with conservatives by bringing up the ways that you sometimes have an appreciation of the moral frameworks they tend to value, and that you tend to de-emphasize.

The following table summarizes some of these differences and the ways that people with different ideologies tend to define these dimensions.[4]

COMMON (NOT UNIVERSAL) DIFFERENCES IN MORAL FRAMEWORKS

Construct	Conservative Moral Framework	Liberal Moral Framework
Harm/Caring (liberals tend to care a lot about this)	Family = Ingroup	Family = Humanity/ Outgroups
Justice/Fairness (liberals tend to care a lot about this)	Achieved, Inherited, Karma, Divinely Destined	Egalitarian/Social Justice/ Meritocratic
Ingroup/Loyalty (conservatives tend to care a lot about this)	Ingroup/Nation	Class/Humanity
Authority (conservatives tend to care a lot about this)	Traditions, Hierarchical Authority, Religious Beliefs	Science, Rational Philosophy, Empiricism
Purity/Sanctity (conservatives tend to care a lot about this)	Traditional Values, Patriotism, Fetuses	Environment, Planet, Women's Body/Choice

Note: Liberals tend to not emphasize the last three frameworks, and they also define them differently when they do emphasize them. The fact that they sometimes care about these dimensions provides you with options for rapport building. In the REACH method's Agree step, you will be encouraged to explore ways you might bring up your appreciation for some conservative frameworks in a way that is honest and helps a conservative conversation partner see you as similar to them.

PRACTICAL IMPLICATIONS

4   Haidt, Jonathan (2013) The Righteous Mind: Why Good People Are Divided by Politics and Religion, New York, Vintage Books, New York

Moral foundations theory can help you adjust your attitude about conservatives and reduce biases you have about them. Reducing your bias is important, because such bias is likely undermining your effectiveness.

In the chapter on the third conversation phase, Agree, I will discuss ways that you might be able to leverage moral foundations theory to build rapport with conservatives. In the chapter on the fourth phase, Coax, I will provide guidance about how to use moral foundations theory to nudge conservatives toward your position on political issues.

> As Dr. King said, "you have very little morally persuasive power with those who can feel your underlying contempt."

IDEOLOGICAL DIFFERENCES ARE NOT JUST ABOUT POLITICS AND MORALITY; THEY ARE ALSO ABOUT LIFESTYLE

As important as these differences in moral frameworks are, Haidt and other social psychologists posit moral ideology is only one aspect of the important differences between the conservative and liberal perspective. Another is a set of key differences that have more to do with a person's lifestyle choices and orientation toward everyday decision-making. Haidt and others argue that a conservative orientation to life values order, routine, similarity, and familiarity. In contrast, a liberal orientation prioritizes novelty, uniqueness, and diversity. According to Haidt, people who identify as conservative tend to like order and predictability. They are not attracted to change for the sake of change, whereas people who identify as liberal usually like to experience variety and diversity.

For many people, reading this may make you quizzical, or even rankle. After all, you may be a very neat person and you don't like having your progressivism questioned. You might go to the same three places for lunch, and always order the same thing. Fair enough, these are just generalizations. But I invite you to do a little thought experiment on the generalities just mentioned to determine if they make some intuitive sense. Imagine:

You are standing at an intersection and witness a minor car accident between two late-model cars. The intersection is in a suburb that is very ideologically mixed. As the drivers open the doors and get out to exchange information, you notice that one driver is wearing a crisp coordinated outfit, has shined shoes, is playing classical music on the radio, and has a car that is spotless and completely undented. As the driver of the other car emerges, you notice that rap music is coming from the car which has a couple of dings, the driver is wearing clothes that could use ironing, with clashing shirt and pants, and you can see a food wrapper on the passenger seat.

Freeze-frame that moment: If you had to guess the political ideology of each person, what would you say?

Most people would guess that the rap-listening dented car driver was a liberal, and the crisp shirt-wearing classical music fan was a conservative. This comports with some generalities that researchers report. As a general proposition, liberals keep their rooms messier than conservatives. We eat different foods, at different restaurants, and revel in variety in a people, vacations, food, culture, music and other aspects of life. So the left/right divide is not just about politics, or even moral values. This divide often involves deep, psychological differences about how we experience the world.

To further illustrate: one study had people report their aesthetic preferences on different patterns of dots moving across a screen. Generally, conservatives liked the images where the dots moved around most in harmony with each other, while liberals preferred patterns that were more chaotic and random.

The following are some general lifestyle differences between conservatives and liberals that Haidt and other social psychologies have researched.

COMMON *(NOT UNIVERSAL)* DIFFERENCES IN PERSONALITY ORIENTATIONS[5]

Common Tendencies Among Liberals	Common Tendencies Among Conservatives
Value Novelty in Experiences *(Travel, Diet, Personal Identification)*	Prefer the Safety and Predictability of Routine and Sameness
See Institutions as Instruments of Caring for People	Value the Stability of Institutions in Themselves
Believe in Change and Risk	Believe in Order and Safety
Often Seek Justice, Even at Risk to Themselves	Often Seek Order, Even at the Expense of the Most Vulnerable
Tend to Question Authority	Tend to Revere Authority
Speak for the Vulnerable	Speak for Institutions
Celebrate Diversity and Flux Among Groups, Not In-Group Membership	Celebrate Loyalty to Groups and Stability Among Them

Clearly, the conservative orientation is not just about politics; it is not even just about underlying moral values. It also is about an orientation to everyday decision-making. It is easy for me to fall into the ideological chauvinism in which I think that my thoroughly liberal worldview is actually superior. Spontaneity rocks! Diversity is good, in food, music, and people! Don't these conservative folks know that it is simply more spiritually evolved to open your heart up to many different types of experiences? What happened to them that they are afraid of differences and new things?

---

5   Haidt, Jonathan (2013) The Righteous Mind: Why Good People Are Divided by Politics and Religion, New York, Vintage Books, New York

Even if in my quiet moments I think that more open minded and open-hearted perspectives are superior, honesty requires that I ask myself two questions:

1. Do I have a bias against the conservative orientation and against conservative people?

2. How might such a bias against the conservative orientation affect the way that conservative people receive my disagreements with them about specific issues?

Progressives need to remember that conservatives are as attached to their orientation toward life as we are to ours. How would you feel if someone presented themselves as trying to have an exchange of views about a specific issue, but you sensed that they actually thought your moral values and even your lifestyle orientation were inferior?

A REASON TO APPRECIATE THE CONSERVATIVE OUTLOOK

In one of his TED talks, Professor Haidt advocates for respect across the ideological divide by reminding us of what he described as the Omnivore's Dilemma, which I will paraphrase:

Humans and other creatures that are omnivores face an interesting dilemma with respect to nutrition, safety, and risk. As an omnivore, their digestive systems can process a wide variety of natural nutrients: insects, other bugs, fruits, vegetables, other plants, sea creatures, and many types of animals. That capacity for variety expands their options for sources of food. On the other hand, there are things in all of those food categories that can sicken, and some that can be fatal. So, what does an individual omnivore or a community of them do when they discover something new that appears to be a potential source of food? This new thing might be the next reliable food source, or it might cause sickness or death.

Different individuals within a group might be resolve this risk/reward dilemma differently. There will be members of the group who are oriented to trying the potential new food source, and others who think best choice for group survival is to stick with the current diet. Over time, different human societies might settle on different ways of resolving this dilemma too, with some being more open to new foods and others much less so.

Now imagine you are part of a nomadic tribe on the savannas of Africa fifty thousand years ago. The tribe has scouts whose role is to roam far from the group looking for water, food sources, and threats. One day the scouts report that they know there is another group of people of a similar size over the horizon. Should your tribe try to approach them in a friendly manner in hopes of forging a useful collaboration? Should your tribe try to avoid them since they may be more powerful and likely to victimize you? Or should your tribe prepare to aggressively confront and perhaps dominate them, because they have resources that your tribe could use?

If we are going to communicate effectively with conservative people, we would do well to remember that the conservative orientation is not evil, but has often served humanity—and us—very well.

No matter how democratic the decision process is, if there is more than one person who influences the decision, there will likely be people whose impulses on this question will pull in different directions. Some people will advocate running from those people, some will say to attack those people, and others will say the tribe should try to join with them. Each of these impulses has survived over the millennia because each of these inclinations has been important to human survival. There are times when personal or group survival is best fostered by rejecting the new thing because it can be harmful (the conservative impulse), and there are also times when it is best to embrace the possibilities of the thing (the liberal impulse). Human societies that survived likely did so because they found a way to make sure that over the long run, the impulse to embrace possibilities and the one to reject new things that might be threats have balanced themselves over many, many decisions.

As human civilization advanced, maintaining a reasonable balance between the conservative and liberal orientations remained important. It is also useful to remember that there are undoubtedly accomplishments that human societies would not have created without a widespread adoption of values related to the conservative viewpoint. Tremendously large-scale projects such as the pyramids in Egypt or South America, Stonehenge, the Roman road system, the Great Wall of China were not built because every person received a somewhat fair wage in a mostly market economy that included labor and capital. A major reason why societies could cooperate at such a large scale to create these wonders was because substantial numbers of people were motivated by loyalty to deities and to royalty (authority), the fidelity to the group (loyalty), and the desire to keep groups uncontaminated by outside forces (purity).

Personally, my personality includes all the hallmarks of progressivism, from the lifestyle choices to the moral values and the policy preferences. My shoes always need a shine, my car needs to be vacuumed, and my computer's desktop is a laughable jumble. If I liked bumper stickers, my first choice would probably say "Question Authority," and the second might be "Co-exist," since I want everybody to see all human beings and most animals (even the ones that people love eating) as the group to which they are loyal. I think the five-second rule for picking up food dropped on the floor is <u>way</u> too restrictive. (A little dirt never hurt!)

Despite all of my liberal orientation proclivities, I can admit that the values of authority, loyalty, and purity have been vital in creating the civilization that I have benefited from. The road systems I drive on, the planes I fly on, and the computer I am writing on represent civilizational accomplishments built on all that has come before, and these would not have been created without a substantial number of people adhering to the conservative point of view that I find constraining to my spirit.

When I remember this, it becomes easier not to look contemptuously at the conservative person who has frames of reference that feel like the complete opposite of mine.

CHAPTER 3

THE R.E.A.C.H. METHOD:
A BEST PRACTICE FOR CONNECTING AND PERSUADING

This chapter will review some findings about best practices for communicating in ways that reduce tensions and increase persuasiveness when people disagree. It will also introduce the REACH method of managing a conversation with someone you disagree with, based on these best practices.

PERSUASION IS NOT ABOUT FACTS

Over the past fifteen years, cognitive scientists have increasingly discussed the finding that introducing people to new facts or concepts is usually not an effective method of persuasion. Facts are not merely ineffective in trying to persuade people from positions that are deeply meaningful to them; when presented with contradicting facts, people's most common response is to deepen their commitment to their belief. Presenting people with facts that contradict their own beliefs only makes them cling to those ideas more fervently—thus the term "backfire effect" was coined to describe this phenomenon.

The popularization of the term "fake news" by President Trump has provided American culture with a shorthand so that people can explicitly reject information that is presented as fact but contradicts their deeply held beliefs. That many conservatives use this term to bolster their denials of climate change or of legitimate findings by credible journalists may lead you to think that the backfire effect is more prevalent among conservatives. In truth, scientists have not noticed a discernible difference between liberals and conservatives in their likelihood of being affected by the backfire effect.

Bottom line: When trying to persuade someone, don't focus on facts that contradict their perspective.

BEING LISTENED TO EMPATHETICALLY HELPS PEOPLE LISTEN TO OTHERS EMPATHETICALLY

In recent years, scientists who study empathy made an unexpected discovery. Social psychologists were examining the conditions under which Israeli Arabs engaged in an empathetic response to stories of Palestinian-Arab suffering. The scientists discovered that one powerful way the researchers could increase the empathetic response to stories of Palestinian suffering was to make sure that the Israeli Arabs had a chance to tell stories of their own suffering first. Subsequent research has suggested that this is not just a one-time finding.

Bottom line: When trying to persuade someone to increase their openness to your point of view, first listen to what they have to say—preferably in the form of their personal experiences.

MIRROR NEURONS AND THE POWER OF STORIES

In the last several decades, brain scientists have concluded that there is an often-engaged cognitive function wherein one person's brain state emulates what they perceive to be the brain state of another person with whom they feel identified. Most people have seen this in action when tears, laughter, or yawning becomes contagious and spreads to people who are not initially sad, mirthful, or sleepy. Brain researchers often use the term "mirror neurons" to describe the part of the brain that gets activated to create this replication effect in one person's brain from what is happening in another person's brain.

While the strength of mirror neurons varies substantially between people, the way to best maximize this effect is to interact in ways that build rapport with the other person so that they identify with you. Demonstrating that you like them and consider yourself part of the same group are both strategies that can help you build rapport and connection in your conversations. One of the best ways of doing this is to tell them a compelling story that has you at the center. Studies of brain scans of storytellers and listeners show that in cases when listeners report a story to be compelling, the listeners' brains light up in the same region as the storytellers'—thus the term mirror neurons.

Bottom line: by honing our stories and telling them to others, we increase the chances that they will understand why we see things like we do.

THE RECIPROCITY PRINCIPLE CAN BE LEVERAGED

Behavioral psychologists have noticed that humans and many other mammals have evolved a consistent pattern of behavior that involves individuals reciprocating beneficial actions that other members of their group have made. This is the part of us that feels obliged to put someone on our holiday card list if we receive one from them or to invite people to our celebrations if they invited us to theirs. We know that we should do unto others as they have done to us.

Bottom Line: If you ask someone to tell a story and listen to them, many people will be inclined to ask you for your experience in return. Even if they don't ask for your story, most people will feel obligated to listen to if you bring up an experience since you have already listened to theirs.

To summarize the implications of these findings:
- Don't try to persuade through facts.
- Focus the conversation on storytelling.
- Let the other person tell their story first.
- Work on your storytelling, so the other person strongly identifies with you when you tell your story.

In addition to some findings from neuroscience and social psychology, there are some important findings from researchers who study conflict resolution about the nature of persuasion that are relevant to cross-ideological conversation. Here are the core findings:

- Become more centered and less reactive.
- Stop being condescending, shaming, angry, and mean.
- Spend energy to find points of alignment and/or agreement.
- Be patient, look at incremental progress positively, but do not expect instant conversions.

These eight principles will be the key ideas behind the REACH method that is explored next.

THE REACH METHOD

The acronym REACH stands for Reflect, Enquire, Agree, Coax, and Honor. The following four chapters of the book explore each step in more depth and give guidance about concrete steps you can take if you want to shift your conversational approach to this best practice method.

Reflect – taking internal steps to maximize your ability to stay calm, centered, and in a position to keep the conversation in the realm of mutual storytelling and empathetic listening.

Enquire – a fancy word (and British spelling) for asking questions. Your goal early in the conversation is to ask your conversation partners not only to clarify their beliefs, but more importantly, to convey on underlying value or experience that drives them to their belief. Naturally, it only makes sense to ask such questions if you have prepared yourself to listen empathetically.

Agree – To build rapport with people, you want to demonstrate that you don't completely dismiss them or their point of view. Your goal is to help them see that there is some degree of alignment or agreement between you, even is the alignment is only partial.

Coax – This is the step where you try to influence people to see that your point of view is based on values they share or an experience they can relate to.

Honor – To put a bow around the conversation, try to get the person to see that you both have values or experiences that can be respected which embody a piece of truth about the issue being discussed.

SOME ADDITIONAL NOTES ABOUT THE REACH METHOD

Ideally, these steps happen in the order specified. However, it is important not to be overly rigid about this. There may be times when your conversation partner asks you a question about your experience, and it would be awkward to refuse to answer them and turn the question back to them.

It is very important to resist the temptation to immediately go to the Coax step where you are trying to influence them. Our natural tendency when talking to people with whom we disagree is to immediately focus on reasons why they need to feel differently, which really means why they are wrong. The mnemonic ABC can help you remember a good rule for how to approach any conflict: Agree Before Challenging.

People don't like to feel as though you are running a program on them. Your goal is to make the conversation feel as natural as possible. The more you practice this method, the better you will be at making it not feel like a scripted method to people you are talking to.

BROTHAMAN SEZ — THE SEARCH FOR A CURE

After my White Ally Toolkit workshops, I often offer to buy a drink or appetizer for anyone willing to give me a video testimonial; usually a few folks take me up on this. Just after the drinks had come at one of these post-workshop sessions, I opened the conversation by conveying my confusion about the way that many white progressives have broken off relationships with old friends, in-laws, cousins and even siblings over politics. After a slightly awkward silence in the group one of the participants said: "I think it's all about E.D.D." we all looked at each other, waiting for the next line.

"We white people have Empathy Deficit Disorder," he said. " I wish there was a pill for it."

I almost spit out my drink.

He was one of the rare white people who seemed to understand that the way that white people are willing to disown or disavow people is not universal, and may be a cultural weakness. I know that I am not the only black person who is alternately flummoxed and inwardly judgmental about the way that white progressives seem disturbingly willing to cut family ties over an electoral vote outcome.

Another time, I was having a wonderfully pleasant breakfast with a white foundation officer friend I had known for a few years. She told me that she had decided that she was not going to talk to specific family members until after President Trump is out of office. I wanted to get on top of my chair and holler:

"WHAT IS WRONG WITH YOU PEOPLE?! DID BEING THE GROUP IN POWER FOR HUNDREDS OF YEARS SCAR YOUR SOULS THAT MUCH??!! YOU PLAYED WITH YOUR COUSIN AS A CHILD AND USED TO LIKE HIM! ARE YOU REALLY GOING TO THROW THAT AWAY BECAUSE OF THE ORANGE CHEETO IN THE WHITE HOUSE?? REALLY??!!"

I did not do this, of course (I liked her, and foundation officers are important folks to have as friends if you do culture change work), but I want white folks in America to consider the possibility that their willingness to disavow social and family contacts might be a culturally specific characteristic, and maybe not a good one. If you have a friend of color whom you can have honest conversations about cultural tendencies with, ask them about this. You will likely create a useful conversation.

More importantly, I encourage white folks to consider this willingness to disavow family is dysfunctional to the collective health of white people, as well as unhealthy for you individually. I am pretty sure this tendency is not helpful to the progressive movement. Some of those folks you are refusing to talk to might be persuadable.

I have to be careful not to become too high and mighty about black folks' ability to navigate political differences among families. It could be that our dialogue and compassion abilities are just not tested as much. Only 8% of black folks voted for President Trump, so very few of us have to figure out how to get through a family reunion with someone wearing a MAGA hat.

But I do think that black folks have learned how to have deep disagreements with family members and still look at them as family. Racial oppression has made it necessary to learn this skill. And of course, my observation about cultural differences on disavowing people, even if true, clearly has some limits. Certainly, family estrangements happen among black folks (though I would love to see research comparing rates of this).

All in all, it seems that white progressives would do well to ask themselves: am I too quick to throw away people I am connected to if I don't like how they think? To paraphrase a workshop I attended at the White Privilege Conference, you can't unfriend everybody.

CHAPTER 4

REFLECT: GETTING READY TO BE EFFECTIVE

If you are going to have a fighting chance at creating a productive encounter with a conservative/Trump supporter, it is vital that you go into the conversation with some measure of inner calm and peacefulness. By the nature of this exchange, the person is likely to say things that you disagree with, or that you will find upsetting. In order for their words to not have power over you, it is important that you work on your ability to relax and calm down, which will make it easier to manage the conversation as you intend.

> Your goal is not to listen like a lawyer looking for flaws in your opponent's logic, ready to pounce on flawed arguments and rhetorical weaknesses.

In addition to calming down, it is useful to ready your spirit for listening empathetically. Your goal is to build rapport—thus, when you are listening, your objective is to listen empathetically, to make your conversation partner feel truly heard, and to find opportunities in what they say that you can follow up on and show alignment with them.

Think of the abilities to calm down and the ability to focus on listening empathetically as muscles that you can train so that at the right time, you can do what is necessary. This chapter provides exercises that many participants have told me are useful for developing these muscles, so you will be better able to engage in the midst of an encounter.

METHODS FOR GETTING CALM AND CENTERED

People take vacations, in part, because they need time to work through disquiet and concerns so that they can operate from a centered place. It is possible to develop the ability to rapidly find a place of calm centeredness from which you can make strategic choices. In the context of engaging conservatives, the skill of becoming calm is important. Sometimes you will unexpectedly fall into a conversation with a conservative that you did not anticipate. Thus, it is useful to know what methods of quick relaxation work for you. If you have explored which methods work well, you can potentially enact one of these methods when needed.

The following are four popular methods that workshop participants told me they have used successfully to gather themselves so they can make good conversation choices.

RELAXATION METHODS
DEEP BREATHING AND NOTICING THOUGHTS
Get in a relaxed sitting position in the quietest place that is convenient to access. Focus on your breathing. When you inhale, think "I am"; when you exhale, think "at peace." As extraneous thoughts come in—and they almost certainly will—notice them, gently push them aside, and return attention to your breathing.

IMAGINE A RELAXING SPOT AND GO THERE

Pick a setting that you find relaxing, whether it is a location you have already been or a place that you can imagine. Spend the first 15 seconds establishing a pattern of relaxed breathing, then close your eyes and shift your attention from your breathing to your preferred location. Imagine as many details as about it as possible, but don't pressure yourself to create the clearest mental picture. Focus on the things about the setting that relax you, whether those are sights, sounds, smells, sensations, or something else. Imagine that you are there and try to live in the relaxation that this place fosters within you.

PROGRESSIVE BODY RELAXATION

During this exercise, you will slide your attention all over your body. At each major body part, take note of how tense or relaxed the part is and try to relax it. Notice how it feels, then move on to the next. Start with your toes and feet, then move up to your ankle, calf, going ever higher and making sure you focus on both sides of your body.

SELF-MASSAGE

Close your eyes. Using your index and middle fingers, make small circles on each temple. Let your fingers walk up your hairline, making small circles along the way, until they reach the middle of your forehead. Then have them travel down until you reach your eyebrow line and make the same circles outward as you head back to your temples. Since hands can carry a lot of tension (especially for heavy keyboarders), do the following: Use the thumb and forefinger to massage the soft area between the thumb and index finger. Do one hand with the other and then switch.[6]

LEARNING WHICH METHODS WORK BEST FOR YOU

For a few days in a row, take time in a relaxed place, and do one of the relaxation methods. Pay attention to how much it affects you. Once you have noticed its usual impact on you, shorten the time of doing the method by one minute. Your goal is to find an effective method that you can do quickly, such as the duration of a trip to the restroom in the midst of a conversation.

You should not wait until you are in a conversation with a conservative before trying these methods. After practicing them in the quiet of your own solitude and knowing which is your favorite, engage it when you are on the verge of a tension-producing conversation on a non-political topic. When you see tension coming, excuse yourself, find a quiet place and practice a relaxation method. The place you go to may be far from optimal, such as a bathroom stall.

---

6 This is from Giovanni Zanoni, Massage Therapist at on-demand massage service, ZenNow

GINNING UP YOUR ABILITY TO LISTEN

As noted earlier, our modern culture emphasizes expression and reaction, but not deep listening. Fortunately, there are specific things that people have found effective for helping them draw their attention and focus to listening. The Listening Tip worksheet includes eighteen tips that workshop participants have told us are useful in this regard.

The tips are in three categories. The first tips focus on managing your own thoughts. These tips are particularly useful before a conversation or at the very beginning of the exchange. Tips in the second category focus on the mind/body connection and include strategies such as what you should do with your gaze or your body position. These can be particularly useful in the midst of an encounter. Tips in the final category concern ways to stay engaged in empathetic listening even though person's viewpoint is something you don't like. These methods can be especially useful when you notice yourself drifting back toward your habitual reactions to what your conservative conversation partner is saying.

> Listening empathetically is key to building the rapport with someone that is necessary to influence them.

My suggestion is that you start experimenting with these strategies in low-tension settings. Every tip does not work equally well for each person, so your goal is to try several of them, and take note of which ones have the greatest effect on you.

BROTHAMAN SEZ —
DON'T HATE THE PLAYER, HATE HIS GAME

When I was a kid, I had a conversation with my mom about a relative she often had tension with beneath the surface of their Southern politeness. After she said something negative about this person, I said, "Mama, I am not surprised you are talking like this. You told me before you did not like her." She paused, then took pains to really emphasize her response in a way that I knew that it was important for me to remember.

"I never said I did not like her," she said. "I said I did not like her ways."

Over the years, I have heard other black people use this same linguistic construct of "not liking someone's ways" to demur from the idea that they did not like someone as a person. When I think about it, this little turn of phrase seems to do a lot of psychological and even philosophical work with incredible efficiency.

Compassion Transforms Conflic

Making this distinction seems to both call upon compassion and generate it. If I separate "the person" and "their ways", then every person becomes redeemable, since everyone can change their ways. No matter what the person is doing and what I think should be done in response, the "dislike the person" versus "dislike their ways" distinction keeps open the possibility of the person's inherent goodness. It also forces me to think about the idea that their unpleasant behavior may be a function of a number of circumstances, some of which they did not control. And this thought implicitly raises the question of how I might fit within this process of circumstances negatively affecting people.

There but for the grace of God go I.

I have done no research about African American vernacular English, so I have no idea about the history of this subtle but powerful turn of phrase. But I do know that there are more than a few black folks who have noticed this phrase is not uncommon. It seems clear to me that this is a linguistic and psychological tool that helps my resilience when dealing with problematic people. If someone is behaving in ways that bother me, my natural tendency is to see their fundamental character as the cause. (In social psychology, this widespread tendency is called the fundamental attribution error, which has been sometimes called a foundational concept of the field of social psychology.) But if I reframe my distaste as being focused on their behavior, I feel a slight boost of energy. Maybe I can influence their behavior, or maybe it will eventually change. Moreover, the distaste just weighs on my heart a little less when I am disliking a person's behavior instead of disliking them.

Thanks mom, for passing this tool down to me.

LEARNING WHICH LISTENING TIPS WILL WORK BEST FOR YOU

Set your phone alarm for a time during the day when it is likely to be easy to get into a conversation (such as lunchtime at work). When your alarm rings, commit yourself to using a listening tip at the start of your next conversation. If possible, extend the conversation to give yourself more time to use a second listening tip. At the end of the conversation, jot a few notes down about how the tips affected you.

Next, commit yourself to using a listening tip when notice your attention wandering during a conversation. Choose one or two tips that you will try to employ. When the moment happens, engage the tactic that you have chosen. Pay attention to how it improves your attention and listening.

QUESTIONS TO ASK YOURSELF BEFORE YOU ENGAGE THE REFLECT STEP

1. What are times when I could likely follow through on my commitment to practicing these methods?

2. Are there people whom I can recruit to remind me that I should engage these methods?

3. Are there topics of conversation that are likely to come up soon that might be useful prompts for me to engage with these methods?

QUESTIONS TO ASK YOURSELF AFTER YOU ENGAGE THE REFLECT STEP

1. What lessons did I learn about settings and moments for engaging these methods?

2. What lessons did I learn about how much or how little impact the lessons had on my spirit and behavior?

GUIDANCE FOR PRACTICE GROUPS

Unless your group is highly motivated by meditative practices, I suggest that you consider having your second group meeting be one where people are expected to discuss their experience with both the Reflect and Enquire steps. Generally, people will be more energized if their practice group meetings include reports about experiences engaging other people instead of just finding moments of calm and relaxation.

It is also a reasonable choice to have one meeting for each step of the REACH method. One advantage of doing so is that the group has more time to recruit additional participants to join the group before people start practicing engagement steps. If you choose to have a group meeting where the homework only focuses on the Reflect step, here are some additional questions to discuss besides the individual ones above:

QUESTIONS FOR GROUP DISCUSSION

1. If you practiced the methods, what impact did this experience have on you?

2. What would be the best way to talk to progressives who enjoy getting angry about conservatives about the benefit of using these methods?

CHAPTER 5

ENQUIRE: ASKING QUESTIONS THAT BUILD RAPPORT AND TRUST

If you are going to influence someone, it is important that you make them feel like you understand where they are coming from. That means asking them questions they will find engaging that also advance your agenda of building rapport. In order to do that, I suggest you ask one or two questions about their belief(s), but don't focus on that for too long. Lingering in the restatement of their beliefs too long re-entrenches them in the own position and is likely to grate on your nerves. Your best bet is to move toward questions that shift their attention to a value or an experience that underlies their belief.

The discussion of values or experiences moves both of you closer to a heart-based interaction and is more likely to fire up the mirror neurons in you both. Talking about values or experiences will likely help you let go of contempt or biases you have about conservatives and will help create a sense of rapport, mutual regard, and perhaps trust.

If you are intuiting that this may be hard for you, know that you are not alone. Upon hearing a conservative perspective, progressives are often very quick to begin a response of explicit refutation, perhaps with an extra dose of condescension thrown in. Alternatively, liberals often respond with an initial question that is actually the start of an interrogation intended to eventually "prove" to the person that their views are wrong. The REACH approach is different. Your goal in the Enquire step is to elicit comments from the person that will help you understand more about how and why they came to those conclusions.

Broadly speaking, there are two approaches to the Enquire step. One is to focus on values behind their statement, and the other is to focus on experiences that led them to their conclusion. Both of these approaches to the Enquire step can be helpful in building rapport during your encounter, but they function somewhat differently.

THE PRIMARY FOCUS TOPIC OF ENQUIRE: VALUES OR EXPERIENCES

Conversations about either values or experiences almost always build more rapport than discussions based on beliefs and facts. When someone expresses a conservative view and you are going to engage them, it often makes sense to ask one or two questions to give them a chance to further elaborate on their beliefs. But you don't want to them to focus on this for too long. Your goal is to get them to shift their focus to what lies beneath their belief, which is either in the domain of values or that of experiences.

Frequently, people can find agreement on a value, even though they disagree about what should happen to best serve this value. Conservatives and progressives often have very different ideas about how the world works and may come to different conclusions about what the government, institutions, or people should do, though they share common values.

For instance, many conservative people favor the gun rights position because they believe this contributes to more personal safety; this same concern about safety also drives many liberal folks' position favoring gun control. Similarly, some conservatives favor the relaxation of government regulations because they want entrepreneurs to have opportunity for business creation and growth, and they think regulations stifle this freedom. At the same time, many liberals favor regulations because they think that such regimes prevent abuse by corporations and give room for aspiring entrepreneurs. In each of these examples, liberals and conservatives share the same underlying value, but have different theories that lead them to opposite policy preferences.

> Hearing about the value(s) beneath a belief—defined as some larger principle that matters to them that is not limited to the specific topic you are discussing—can be helpful to rapport building.

By getting your conservative conversation partner to talk about the values underlying their belief, you open up possibilities to demonstrate agreement/alignment with them, which is the next step in the REACH method.

METHODS FOR ASKING ABOUT VALUES

Method 1: "I bet there is something you care about deeply that drives your take on this? What is that?" Because people in our argumentative culture don't typically ask such questions, it is sometimes useful to let them know that you are not trying to trap or trick them. One way of doing this is to explain/justify why you are asking about their values. Here are three ways of doing this:

Method 2: "I recently read something from an expert about reducing the polarization. He said that it's often good to ask about what people care about that is driving their opinion. So: what is a value you hold that is linked to why you see it this way?" *(justify using an expert)*

Method 3: "You sound really passionate about this. I have found that when I am listening to someone's views, it can really help me to hear about a value they care about that is underneath their belief. So, I want to ask, what is something you care deeply about that leads to the position you have?" *(justify using your own experience)*

Method 4: "I am curious about something you care about that is underneath this. It looks like (or I have found that) people who favor gun restrictions and those who hate gun restrictions both feel the way they do because they value safety. What is something you value related to this?" *(justify with provocative mini teaching)*

METHODS FOR ASKING ABOUT EXPERIENCES

As valuable as it can be to focus the Enquire step on values, it may be even more powerful to focus on experiences. As a general matter, there is a special power that storytelling about experiences has for helping build rapport between people. By getting the person to tell you about an experience that is linked to their conclusion, you put yourself in a position to fire up your and your conversation partner's mirror neuron circuitry. You may feel connected to them as they tell your story, and if you are listening empathetically, they may feel this connection too. This only helps your future attempts to get to them to see things from your point of view.

Sometimes, people have difficulty probing their minds for experiences related to their beliefs, so you may need to be both patient and supportive of the other person probing their memory banks for a story. (Of course, sometimes people don't really have a story related to their belief; it will be important to not shame them for this or use this as evidence they are "wrong.") Because people are not used to being authentically asked for their experience, it can be useful to frame your probe in a way that feels natural and not part of a rhetorical trap.

Three different ways of asking for relevant experiences vary by the time horizon of the question. The following are examples of frames that focus on current/recent experiences, past experiences, or their development path over time.

Method 5: "I would love to hear about an experience you have had in the past couple years that re-enforces how you see this issue." *(recent focus)*

Method 6: "That is an interesting way of seeing that. I would love to hear about an experience that you had that helped you first see things this way." *(past focus)*

Method 7: "I am often curious about how people's views of these things linger or change. Could you tell me about how your views of these issues have evolved over time and some things you have seen that have affected your point of view?" *(developmental focus)*

One question that progressives usually raise in response to guidance about the Enquire step is what happens if they respond to your Enquire move by quoting Rush Limbaugh, Breitbart News, or some other conservative media outlet?

It is very common for people to respond to values or experience questions not by answering them, but instead repeat information that they have received from the media. It is important to be prepared for this and not let it frustrate you into reverting to an argumentative approach, no matter how much contempt you have for the news source. If this happens, I suggest that you take a deep breath, remind yourself that it is unproductive to criticize them or their media sources, and commit to trying to refocus your partner on your actual question. Here are two slightly different ways of motivating them to answer your question after they have referenced some right-wing media source in response to your question on values or experience:

Response 1: Compliment them for being news consumers, then refocus on their value/experience underneath their viewpoint, then express confidence that they probably ground their beliefs in actual experiences.
What this might sound like:
It's great that you are a good news consumer. But there is so much bad media out there. I bet you would not believe things in the media if they did not align with some experience you have had. So, I am still interested in your experiences (or values) that line up with what the media source said.

Response 2: Raise the issue of their influence on you.
What this might sound like:
That is interesting that you heard that in the media. I have found though, that I am more likely to be affected by a point of view if I understand the values (or experiences) that exists in people's hearts or their history.

PRACTICING THE ENQUIRE STEP

Even though everyone has asked people questions, only a small portion of the population have jobs based on forming and asking questions (examples include lawyers, investigators, and mental health counselors). Otherwise, most people have not done focused work on their question-asking skills. Like many things, the task of asking questions has elements of art in that some people have natural talents, and it also has some characteristics of skill in that that anyone can get better through intentional practice.

Asking good, non-confrontational questions when you are also trying to contain your reaction to someone whose opinions enrage you is an additional challenge for most progressives. So how do you build up the capacity to do it?

In my multi-week workshops, I give people homework and encourage them to focus on one or two additional skills during interactions before the next session. This allows people to learn one step at a time, and practice progressively each skill of the REACH method as the workshop progresses. Since people have different levels of both skill and engagement, it is useful to give participants homework assignments that are likely to challenge people to different extents. For practicing the Enquire step, here are four levels of difficulty that you might attempt before you move to the Agree step that is explored in the next chapter.

ENGAGING ENQUIRE METHODS AT DIFFERENT LEVELS OF DIFFICULTY

LEVEL 1

Ask an experience or values question after someone you usually agree with expresses an opinion that you mostly agree with. If asking questions and patiently listening is not something you do frequently, you may start with a topic that is not even politically related. For example: "I also really like going to Austin, Texas. Tell me about something that happened to you on your last visit that confirmed why you like it so much."

LEVEL 2

Ask an experience or values question to another progressive about a topic that you know you disagree about. For example: "I know that you and I disagree about drug legalization. I am curious about a value you hold that influences your perspective on this."

LEVEL 3

Ask a conservative person about a topic that you likely disagree on, but that is not a political topic. For example: "I know that you go to one of the same four restaurants every day for lunch. I am very different—I am always trying to find new places. I am interested in knowing how you discovered you prefer going to familiar places over always looking for something new to experience."

LEVEL 4

Raise a political topic with a conservative likely to have an opposing viewpoint. After they tell you how they feel, ask them to tell you about a value or experience that might be driving their belief. For example: "A few months ago, we had a conversation about gun control. I realize that I did not ask you about any experiences you had that are related to how you see this. Would you mind sharing one?"

Before you start the conversation, make a preliminary decision about whether you are going to tell your conversation partner that you are asking them the question as part of a skill-building exercise. If you do so, people will generally give you grace and answer the question, but their reaction to you (and maybe what they say) will be less natural. In the long run, you will want to approach such encounters naturally and not give such provisos. But if you are nervous or if your partner appears to find the question off-putting, mentioning that you are intentionally working on asking questions can be helpful to smoothing over the moment.

Another choice to make as you are practicing these skills is how willing you would be to express your own opinion if they ask about it. In most cases, people can do better reflection on this exercise as a learning process if they just listen to the other person, and leave it at that. However, if your conversation partner asks your perspective and you think demurring would make the moment feel weird, express your perspective, preferably through a focus on values or experience. If you want a way out of expressing your opinion, one option is to tell the person that you are working on your listening skills. Express your willingness to tell them your point of view at some other time.

QUESTIONS TO THINK ABOUT BEFORE YOU ENGAGE THE ENQUIRE STEP:

1. At what level of difficulty do you plan to engage?

2. What topics, people, and settings do you plan to engage?

3. What might be some issues that you aspire to talk about after you have worked on your skills on the "easy" issues?

4. Are there people to whom you have access who would be particularly useful to practice Enquire tactics on? On what topics that you could engage them?

5. Are there people whom you should probably avoid engaging until after you have become more skilled in these tactics?

6. Which question method(s) are you planning to use?

7. Which relaxation methods or listening tips do you plan to engage?

QUESTIONS TO THINK ABOUT AFTER YOU ENGAGE THE ENQUIRE STEP:

1. Looking back on it, what positive or negative lessons did you learn about your choice of topic, person, and setting?

2. How did your relaxation methods and/or listening tips affect your performance as an empathetic listener?

3. Did you ask about values or experience? Why did you choose that approach?

4. Was there anything notable about the person's reaction to being asked to go beneath their belief?

5. Did the person say anything that struck or surprised you?

6. What did you notice about your ability to conduct the asking and listening exercise?

GROUP DISCUSSION QUESTIONS:

1. Were there settings you passed over that might have been fruitful? Were there settings that were suboptimal that maybe you should have not engaged?

2. Given our individual lessons about choosing settings, are there any collective lessons about choosing settings, people, or topics?

3. What does the variation in the effect of the relaxation methods and listening tip on us tell us about this practice? Are there any generalized lessons that we need to note collectively?

4. What generalizations can be made about the effect of asking about values/experiences in conversations with conservatives?

5. How do you feel about your progress toward the goals of: (1) creating encounters that are less tense and (2) becoming more persuasive? Are you more enthused, somewhat discouraged, or having some other reaction?

CHAPTER 6

AGREE: BUILDING RAPPORT AND TRUST THROUGH HIDDEN ALIGNMENT

The Agree step is probably the hardest step for anyone who is trying to use best practice methods of persuasion; our psyches have evolved to see people we disagree with as a threat that needs to be defeated. Finding and focusing on agreement is particularly difficult for white progressives, even when their potential conversation partner is someone they love. (See BrothaMan's comments in this chapter.) From the standpoint of building rapport, the Agree step is probably more important than the Enquire step. It is by demonstrating agreement and alignment that you lower your conversation partner's defenses.

The Agree step actually includes two phases: the intellectual task of finding the basis of agreement, and perhaps the more difficult emotional task of mobilizing our will to do so. The purpose of the Reflect step is to reconnect you to a place of center where you can (1) reconnect to your goals of connection and persuasion, and (2) remember that temporarily letting go of your inclination to view the person as an enemy serves those goals. In the Agree step, your task is to make a choice from this centered place to look for, find, and then express a level of agreement with your conversation partner's conservative viewpoint that you otherwise oppose.

> When progressives engage conservatives, they are often so agitated by the conversation that they forget (or refuse to do) basic rapport-building strategies.

Let's assume that the calm that you created in the Reflect step has been maintained, even though hearing their answers to the questions you asked in the Enquire step was upsetting. If you did the Enquire step correctly, you have at least gotten your conversation partners to talk about some value(s) that are driving their position; perhaps you have gone even further and gotten them to talk about a personal experience that is related to their belief. If you have made them feel deeply heard, they are now feeling somewhat relaxed, and are a bit more confident that they do not have to be at attention and ready to reflexively defend their beliefs. Now it's time to further build on the rapport you have established by showing some agreement and alignment with them.

The options for connecting with them in the Agree phase exist on at least three levels:

1. The atmospherics of the conversation, where you highlight ways that you have similarities with them that may have little to do with the topic at hand

2. Shared values somewhat related to the topic being discussed

3. Your analysis of the complexities of the topic

HIGHLIGHTING ALIGNMENT THROUGH THE ATMOSPHERICS OF THE CONVERSATION

I am using the term "conversation atmospherics" to signify that there are ways to add comments to conversations that are not on the central topic, that remind both people they have similarities as human beings. I think of these atmospheric surface level similarities as falling into three categories: surface similarities, lifestyle similarities and moral similarities.

SURFACE SIMILARITIES

These are the easiest to find and require very little introspection or analysis. One or two well-placed comments that show similarity (like "I also have a grandson.") or admiration (like "I like those shoes, my wife has shoes like that too.") may seem similar to cheap flattery. But experts on persuasion know that these sentiments can play a big role in persuasion.[7] In the difficult work of reducing tension and bridging the left/right chasm, this level of rapport building should not be ignored.

LIFESTYLE AND MORALITY

In chapter 2, I discussed the fact that there is a conservative orientation to the world that is reflected in some lifestyle choices and moral perspectives. It can be useful to drop these similarities into conversations. Remember, a significant part of the human psyche is tribal, and is frequently assessing the degree to which someone appears to be part of their tribe or part of another possibly opposing tribe. The more you can send messages (that seem sincere and not forced) about natural similarities, the more rapport you can build.

One strategy for developing support is to convey that there is a little conservative inside of you. If you notice a sense of revulsion within you at this idea, you might reflect on the possibility of you having an anti-conservative bias worth paying attention to.

The implication of this is that it is useful to do a personal inventory at the level of your lifestyle preferences and morality and look for parts of you that are at least somewhat conservative. It can be helpful to you to drop these tidbits off-handedly in conversation, since doing so will help your conservative conversation partner feel more confident that you are part of their tribe.

SIMILARITIES IN LIFESTYLE

Many progressives have some characteristics that reflect the conservative worldview. Maybe you are a stickler for keeping your car tidy; perhaps you obsess about showing up on time; maybe there are some areas where your disgust reaction is highly attuned. I have provided a worksheet designed to help you think about the ways in which the conservative within you drives some of your lifestyle choices

---

7   Client Denier Roundup, (2020) New Research Points to Effective Ways to Talk to Skeptical Conservatives about Climate Change, www.desmog.com

and preferences. The next time you are engaging a conservative, you should consider if there are any opportunities to mention that you also admire order, regularity, and structure, or some other conservative preference, just like they do.

The worksheet *Finding Your Inner Conservative: Lifestyle Similarities* encourages you to identify areas of your lifestyle preferences that might be useful to drop in a conversation to aid your rapport building with a conservative.

SIMILARITIES IN APPRECIATION OF CONSERVATIVE MORAL VALUES

Another dimension where you might find conversational atmospherics that build rapport is at the level of moral values. Even if you are a progressive who overwhelmingly emphasizes caring and justice, there may be some characteristics you have or respect that focus on the more commonly held conservative moral values. Bringing these up as side comments to the primary thrust of the conversation can serve you. Some possibilities are illustrated below.

Authority

Even if you might be anti-authoritarian in general, you might maintain a high regard for a religious leader, specific scientist or scientific authority; there might be business leaders you think are particularly worth listening to.

Loyalty

Many progressives are very loyal to their neighborhood, city, or sports team. In addition, there are progressives who appreciate seeing loyalty in others. For instance, on many occasions, white workshop participants have told me they deeply appreciate the loyalty that black members of sororities and fraternities show to these organizations.

Purity

Are there areas where you notice yourself advocating for purity or feeling disgust when purity is violated? For instance, I personally feel a special kind of disgust when I come across litter in outdoor public spaces like national parks. Maybe you are a hardcore vegan that is disgusted by a rare steak. The opportunity is to become familiar with domains where you value the purity and sanctity of things and consider bringing these up in conversation when it might be helpful to rapport building.

The worksheet *Finding Your Inner Conservative: Moral Frameworks* encourages you to do some self-reflection on areas of life in which you may express placing a value on these conservative frameworks. After you find these areas, you can practice bringing up these facts as asides during conversations about other issues.

WHAT MIGHT IT LOOK LIKE TO REFERENCE THE CONSERVATIVE WITHIN YOU?

Suppose that you are in a conversation about police and community relations with a conservative. They may be more worried about too many constraints on police, and you are worried about insufficient police accountability. After you ask them about an experience that reinforces their sense that the more pressing problem is constraints on police, you are going to offer your perspective. Your tactic may be to first tell a story about a good encounter with a police officer (Agree step) before you tell another story that highlights the problem of police abuse (Coax step).

Your good cop story might involve an anecdote about being pulled over by a police officer. As you describe the encounter, you might describe your attitude of compliance as the officer approached you, **not** based on fear and resentment of police authority, but rather respect and appreciation for their devotion to public service and the dangers police officers endure. In truth, both of these emotions might have been activated within you, but your intention is to tell the story in a way that maximizes the conservative's identification with you. If your car is a place you keep clean and orderly, you might add that small detail to your story. These references to appreciation for authority as well as orderliness support your efforts to move your conversation partner to trusting you and your perspective. This will help you when you get to tell your story where you try to Coax them to a new point of view.

FINDING YOUR INNER CONSERVATIVE: LIFESTYLE SIMILARITIES

WHAT ARE SOME PERSONAL CHARACTERISTICS YOU CAN BRING UP IN A CONVERSATION TO HELP A PERSON SEE YOU AS PART OF THEIR TRIBE? THESE ARE THINGS YOU MIGHT BRING UP AS ASIDES IN A CONVERSATION:

Examples:

- I like predictability and similarity in my vacation planning. (sameness/predictability)

- Keeping my car neat and clean (or my bed made up) is very important to me. (order)

- When my pastor/priest expresses an opinion, I give it a lot of weight. (authority)

Characteristic 1:

Characteristic 2:

Characteristic 3:

FINDING YOUR INNER CONSERVATIVE: MORAL FRAMEWORKS

Try to think about specific situations where your thoughts or actions demonstrated you putting value on one of the three moral values that conservatives tend to emphasize. The closer you can get to telling a true statement that will resonate with the way a conservative defines this issue, the stronger a tool you will have.

LOYALTY: WHAT GROUPS DO YOU HAVE A STRONG SENSE OF LOYALTY TO? ARE THERE GROUPS WHOSE SENSE OF LOYALTY YOU ADMIRE?

(e.g. your faith group, your neighborhood, an educational institution, your profession, your family)

Group 1:

Group 2:

AUTHORITY: WHAT ARE SOME TYPES OF AUTHORITY FIGURES YOU HAVE HIGH GENERAL REGARD FOR?

(e.g. religious officials, historical figures, law enforcement, scientists)

Figure 1:

Figure 2:

PURITY: WHAT ARE SOME AREAS WHERE YOUR SENSE OF CRINGE/DISGUST/REVULSION IS ACTIVATED WHEN PURITY IS VIOLATED?

(e.g. bodies of water, forests, flavors, insects in settings where insects are not supposed to be, food choices/ diet, clothing)

Area 1:

Area 2:

BROTHAMAN SEZ – WHO YOU TALKING TO?

In my workshops coaching white anti-racism allies about how to usefully respond to white people who make racially problematic statements, I often discuss how many black folks have engaged a relevant strategy for hundreds of years. This strategy is called code-switching and signifies the idea that one way of maximizing your effectiveness in talking to people is using different communication styles when talking to people who deeply understand your perspective than when speaking to those who don't. This practice goes back to slavery at least, when enslaved people learned that they could better influence white people when they spoke to them in ways much more formal, less emotional, and with a different diction style than what they used when they spoke to each other.

Black folks know that you shouldn't talk to your mama the same way you talk to your sister. In fact, black comedians frequently rely on the comic trope of laughing at white people because of the disrespectful way that their children talk to their parents. What black people are laughing at in these jokes is white people's obliviousness to the importance of code-switching.

Many white progressives would do well to heed the wisdom that code-switching embodies. ***Progressives often use the same language, concepts, and amped up tones when they are talking to conservatives that they use when talking to other progressives. This does not work.*** What brothers and sisters who code-switch know is that there is often a very large gap in assumptions between two people, and if you want to maximize your influence, you need to make sure that you are using language, concepts, facts, and frames of reference that your conversation partner understands, not just ones that you like. Enslaved people understood this, and their descendants who have to navigate white and non-white worlds today often get this. If white progressives want to be more persuasive, they may need to start code-switching too.

AGREEMENT ON VALUES AND POSITIONS

Using the conversational atmospherics just discussed is not unlike a salesperson using flattery and charm before getting around to price and terms. Such strategies can be helpful, but usually at some point you will need to focus attention on the core issues. Similarly, when talking to a conservative, you want to invest energy in finding some level of substantive agreement if you can. I suggest you look for this agreement in two domains: values and positions.

In each case, I strongly suggest that you show agreement with your partner by relating a personal experience that illustrates you have some level of agreement with them. As discussed in chapter 2, telling a reasonably compelling story helps to engage your conversation partner's mirror neurons and build trust.

TELLING STORIES THAT HIGHLIGHT AGREEMENT ON VALUES

> Telling a story that shows alignment at the level of common values helps conservatives see you as a person whom they might be able to trust.

As discussed in the Enquire chapter, one purpose of your questions is to have your partners highlight values that underlie their opinion. Sometimes, your partner will focus on values that are relatively easy to align yourself with. For instance, gun rights advocates might discuss how important it is for them to feel like they can protect their family. People who believe in reducing the social safety net might associate that with their desire to provide a good launch of the young people in their family. While you disagree with them on their views on policy, you probably also believe in protecting your family and launching young adults in the world successfully; you might be able to tell a personal story that illustrates how this value drives your behavior.

Relating a story that demonstrates you share some underlying value is very useful in containing disagreement that is inherent in a conversation between people who disagree on issues. Even a temporary focus on this similarity makes it hard for either of you to excessively focus on negative tensions, because it is clear that you are alike in a domain that matters. Nevertheless, many people will notice that you are not really agreeing with their position on the topic. Sometimes, alignment at the level of values is all you can achieve. In many cases though, if you think about the topic hard enough (and perhaps in advance), you can find a way to clarify that you have some level of agreement (even if it is very narrow) with your conservative conversation partner.

It is best if you convey that you share a common value with them through a story that illustrates you have behaviors or thoughts that reflect this value. Even if the story is not about an action but about your inner thoughts and reflections when you observed something, try to convey the value through a story, since storytelling works best. If you really can't think of a story, just stating that you have a shared value with them is better than not doing so.

TELLING STORIES THAT SHOW SOME AGREEMENT ON POSITIONS

If you focus conversational energy on the common values as just discussed, you will be doing much better than most progressives do in discussions with conservatives. Typically, people just reject the premises and observations of the conservative, and things descend into arguments that don't get anywhere. Still, if your

Agree step only involves you telling a story of common values, some discerning conversation partners will recognize that you have not really said anything about the particular policy you are discussing. An even more effective strategy—but one that is more difficult—is to tell as personal story that conveys that their perspective on the issue has some degree of merit, in at least a few cases.

AN EXAMPLE OF FINDING A SLIVER OF AGREEMENT

To illustrate, let's return to the gun control argument. After recognizing that you disagree with them on this issue, suppose that you ask them for an experience that illustrates why they favor gun rights. Suppose they tell you about a moment in a public situation where they felt some degree of unease, but when they noticed someone who was openly carrying, they became more comfortable.

One potentially powerful way to agree with them is to relate an experience (if you have one) where you also felt safer because of the presence of a firearm. Many people who favor gun control (like me) have had at least one experience where the possession of a gun by someone made them more comfortable. Personally, the reason that I favor gun control is that I think most of the time, the presence of guns held by citizens makes things more tense instead of less. I have had more experiences where the presence of a gun led me to feel less safe.

But that does not prevent me from acknowledging that there have been one or two times when I have directly experienced that the presence of a citizen-owned gun enhanced my sense of safety. If I am in a conversation about gun control and bring up my experience that is aligned with their viewpoint, the person will correctly feel that I am agreeing with them, at least in part. In fact, they are not wrong; I am telling them on purpose that the connection they are drawing between guns and enhanced feelings of safety is not crazy or something to be dismissed. I can decide to feel comfortable doing this because in short order (when I get to the Coax step), I am going to convey another experience that leads to my ultimate conclusion that overall, more guns produce less safety. But for the moment, the person will feel that I am allied with them.

A SECOND ILLUSTRATION

Suppose that I am talking to a conservative who favors drastic reductions in the social safety net on the grounds that such supports make people lazy and breed dependence. As a progressive, suppose that I find this to be a fundamental mischaracterization of what happens the vast majority of time with these supports. In fact, I think that there are people who need help who don't get it, and I also believe that our economic system is far too skewed and creates zillionaires and low wage jobs that people cannot live on. But even though I believe this, I may have had an exceptional experience where I think that the availability of external supports did in fact play a role in keeping someone from getting their work habits and affairs in order. Even if I think that other factors (such as racism or structural unfairness) matter more most of the time, it might be possible for me to authentically agree that social welfare supports sometimes contribute to excessive dependence.

In our highly conflict-oriented culture, we are not taught to make concessions to people we oppose. Even if I have a cousin who I think is abusing disability support systems, I have been trained by liberal culture **never** to admit this to someone who is conservative, because I fear that I would only be validating their skewed beliefs with which I disagree. This hyper-argumentative culture that affects both progressives and conservatives hides from us an important truth that conflict resolution experts know. If I were to tell an anecdote about an experience that I think is unusual and my partner thinks is common, my partner will feel that the "truth" they have pointed out is not something that I am dismissing. This moment of connection not only keeps them relaxed: it also makes it harder for them to summarily dismiss my upcoming story about why safety nets are important.

By finding some agreement, you encourage them to shift from the perspective "I am right and you are wrong" to a more nuanced perspective. Your position is that both of you can be right, and that your position on the issues allows this. This rhetorical technique not only models the kind of thinking you want them to do, but it also engages the reciprocity principle, which is deeply ingrained in human psychology. In this example, if they feel I have granted that they have a piece of the truth, some part of them will feel some pressure to subsequently acknowledge that I have a piece of the truth too.

HOW DO YOU FIND THE PLACE OF AGREEMENT?

What follows is a method for reorienting yourself that often makes it easier to find some level of agreement with another person. It is borrowed from a conversation management strategy called motivational interviewing, which is used by some mental health counselors to help clients connect with their ambivalence about their problematic behavior. It is often used to engage people suffering from addiction; the point is to get people to pay attention to the parts of themselves that are unhappy with their addiction, even if they are mostly enjoying it and are reluctant to change.

Counselors who try to assist people to help them move from dysfunctional behaviors have found that even while people might be deeply committed to self-undermining behaviors, there is a small part of them that feels that these behaviors are something they want to stop. The key to motivational interviewing is to create a conversational setting where the counselor honors the dominant part of the client's perspective, but then creates some room to help the client focus attention on the smaller—and healthier—part of them that wants to stop the problematic behavior.

This method could be used on any issue.

1. Imagine an opinion scale where 0 is neutral on gun control, 100 is so staunchly in favor of gun rights that someone is ready to engage in violent protest to support them; -100 is the mirror opposition position and represents someone who is ready to engage in violent protest to enact the strictest possible gun control measures.

2. Clarify what number represents your position. Conceivably, your number will not be -100.

3. Then, ask yourself, what are the reasons why you are NOT at -100.

Some examples from a gun control advocate about why they are NOT ready to go to war over the issue might be:

POLICY

I think that responsible hunters with "long guns" should be able to pursue their hobby lawfully.

A government program to confiscate firearms would scare me because I don't want to see police powers extended in that way.

VALUES

Within reason, I value people's freedom. This includes the freedom to hunt lawfully, though I don't do that myself.

EXPERIENCES

I have hiked in the wilderness with a guide who was concerned about the group's safety from bears and mountain lions. Though we took many measures to avoid encountering these animals, the guide carried a gun as a last resort. This is responsible possession of a firearm, and I would not want to see it prohibited.

Once you have articulated a reason or two that your opinion is not at -100, you have the basis for creating a sense of agreement with a gun rights advocate. Even though you strongly disagree with them, there is some common ground: you are NOT at -100 and there is a reason for that. The challenge is to articulate this at the right time, in a way that is authentic, and in a way that they know you are not completely dismissing their point of view.

SUMMARY

In this chapter, I have provided multiple levels of options for saying things in a conversation that will demonstrate to a conservative that you have some level of agreement and alignment with them. Given how many ways there are to do this, you may want to prepare in advance for such conversations. Consider choosing one or two issues as well as one or two people whom you will engage for practice.

You can think through all of the Agree approaches outlined in this chapter (conversational atmospherics, values, and positions) in advance of the conversation.

As you engage these strategies, it may be helpful to look at yourself as investing in a skill that you will be using for the rest of your life. No matter what happens in the next election, conservative people will not be going away—and there will be other elections. Without a doubt, you will experience a learning curve with these methods. You will make mistakes, and that is OK. You will be better the fifth time than the first time, and better the twentieth time than the fifth time. The most important thing is to get started.

As you engage these methods, you should consider sometimes skipping forward to the Agree step a few times. The Coax step will involve its own complexities, and it may be better to truly consolidate your learning of the Agree step before you move on. If you do this with conservatives, you may worry about reinforcing their views that you don't like. I would encourage you to permit yourself the latitude to work on your skills in this way. Your ability to achieve mastery of these methods is important in order for you to be the best progressive change agent you can be. Temporarily validating a few conservative folks' views is a worthy sacrifice for this larger goal.

ENGAGING AT DIFFERENT LEVELS OF DIFFICULTY

LEVEL 1

Initiate a conversation with a progressive you know about a non-political topic you disagree about, such as how much you like a particular neighborhood, restaurant, or activity. After having them discuss their experiences of the issues, do your best to find as much agreement/alignment as you can. Don't forget to try to look for and bring up conversational atmospherics that are rapport-building. If possible, bow out of the conversation after the Agree step.

LEVEL 2

Engage a likely conservative person on a topic that is largely apolitical, as above.

LEVEL 3

Engage a progressive friend on a political topic that you know you disagree about. Follow the same steps as above.

LEVEL 4

Identity two conservatives with whom you could easily and non-awkwardly create a conversation. For each, think about a political issue you are likely to disagree about that does not tend to trigger you. Think through how you might approach the person, including what you think would be useful in the Reflect, Engage, and Agree steps. When you have an opportunity, engage them in this conversation. Try to avoid an argument, and unless it would create weirdness, bow out of the conversation after the Agree step. Take good notes on your experience and the lessons you learned.

REFLECTION QUESTIONS BEFORE YOU ENGAGE THE AGREE STEP

1. What are the settings, topics, and methods that are likely to stretch you, but not too much?

2. What are you most nervous/uncertain about as you think about engaging someone?

REFLECTION QUESTIONS AFTER YOU ENGAGE THE AGREE STEP

1. What surprises did this experience involve, positive or negative?

2. How well did the relaxation methods and listening tips affect you?

3. What did you learn from the Agree step, either about yourself or about your conversation partner?

4. How difficult was it to think of and articulate alignment with your conversation partner? Did you experience any emotions that were noteworthy?

5. What lessons were there from what you planned and from what you did?

QUESTIONS FOR GROUP DISCUSSION

1. Given our experiences, how might we improve the instructions for this exercise for ourselves and other people who want to do it?

2. Are there any collective lessons about choosing topics, people, and settings that emerge from looking at all of our experiences?

3. Were there ways of trying to connect that were particularly fruitful or particularly clunky?

CHAPTER 7

COAX AND HONOR:
INVITING OTHERS TO SEE EVERYONE CAN BE RIGHT

At last, you have arrived! To some extent, the Reflect, Enquire, and Agree phases are warm-up acts to the Coax and Honor steps, which are the main events if your focus is on persuasion. To be sure, if a primary objective of yours is to create a peaceful encounter; the first three phrases are central. But many people who crave best-practice methods are focused not just on peacebuilding, but also on moving people's opinion. This is what the Coax and Honor phases focus on directly.

Before going to this central topic, a bit more about the issue of attitude. I mentioned this in chapter 2 but it bears repeating: you need to cultivate a paradoxical relationship with your objective of changing your conversation partner's mind. On the one hand, you are going through this whole process largely because you want to move someone's opinion. Given the dire problems facing this country and the level of divisiveness that is impeding cooperation, it is vital that progressives start becoming more persuasive.

> "Convince a man against his will,
> He's of the same opinion still."
> – Mary Wollstonecraft, British writer, feminist, and mother to the author of Frankenstein

On the other hand, if you are too thirsty for changing the mind of your conversation partners, you will actually undermine your efforts. No one likes to feel like a project, a trophy, or an object. Your efforts to move conservatives to a new position on whatever issue you are discussing will likely be unsuccessful if they experience you as trying to push them. They need to feel like you have invited them to realize something, but you are somewhat indifferent to them being "converted". Essentially, they need to feel like they are changing their opinion for themselves, not because you want them to.

COAX – MAKING AN INVITATION TO TAKE YOUR PERSPECTIVE SERIOUSLY

There are two somewhat overlapping but also distinct approaches to trying to move someone to your opinion:

1. Highlighting how arguments based on conservative moral values can support your progressive position

2. Sharing an experience that aligns with a conservative worldview or value and yet supports a progressive position

These methods can be combined, but I will discuss them separately so that you can see them more clearly.

COAX METHOD 1: USING CONSERVATIVE MORAL ARGUMENTS FOR PROGRESSIVE POSITIONS

This is the more intellectually complex of the two Coax strategies. To use this approach, you will need to resist your natural tendency to link your position on an issue to moral frameworks you value. Instead, your task is to link your position to moral frameworks that you probably only care a little about. This is not only difficult intellectually: it is also challenging emotionally because many progressives have a bias against conservative moral values. Many of us have bumper stickers that say, "Question authority." Many believe that we need to expand our view of who is considered "us." Some of us (e.g. The Society for the Prevention of Cruelty to Animals) are so committed to a broad view of groups that that they believe we should be loyal to many non-human species. Finally, many of us have seen the way that arguments about purity have been used to perpetuate arguments for all-male environments, racially segregated neighborhoods, country clubs that don't admit Jews, and all manner of exclusions.

Though expressing support for these other moral values may not come naturally to us, it is important; there is good research showing that doing so significantly increases persuasiveness. There have been several studies that have examined the effectiveness of arguments for positions and their impact on people by having conservative and liberal people hear arguments against their natural positions.[8] When presented with conservative arguments for conservative positions, progressives were much less likely to be convinced than when they were presented with progressive arguments for conservative positions. The same dynamic happens when scientists reverse the ideological positions and arguments. This is a general finding about language, cognition, and persuasion.

To get to the point where you can effectively use this method of influencing people, you will need to work on your bias against conservative moral touchstones; you will also need to create a situation where you can practice making arguments that don't come to you naturally. For instance, it may be useful to try out these arguments using conservative arguments for progressive positions in practice conversations with other liberals just to get used to hearing these words come out of your mouth. At the end of this chapter, I will give some ideas about how you might practice this method.

The table Conservative Arguments for Progressive Positions reviews several issues and lays out some examples of conservative arguments for progressive positions. Some of these may be harder to swallow than others. Obviously, this table is not comprehensive; it is intended to be illustrative. If you want to use this approach, you will need to do some thinking about issues you are most likely to have conversations with conservatives about, and practice making arguments for those positions using conservative moral frameworks.

8   Cialdini, Robert (2020), Principles of Persuasion, www.influenceatworks.com, Influence at Work: Proven Science for Business Success

The following questions may be helpful in this process:

AUTHORITY

- Is there a record of any sources of authority that a conservative would respect (e.g. God, religious leaders, esteemed political or cultural figures) supporting your position or criticizing the opposite position?
- Is there a way that the policy you favor would have the effect of increasing people's respect for the idea of following authority?
- Is there an argument that the opposite of the policy you favor tends to undermine the sense of authority or the regard for authorities who should be respected?

LOYALTY

- Are there groups that merit loyalty who might benefit from this policy position?
- Are there groups w that merit loyalty ho might be hurt by the opposite of this policy position?
- Is there a way that this policy position has the impact of increasing the sense of loyalty among people generally, or among specific groups?

PURITY

- Is there a way the policy you support will enhance the sense of purity about a place, a population, or something else worthy of thinking about?
- Does the opposing policy contribute to the degradation of something in a way that can be connected to a lack of purity?

CONSERVATIVE ARGUMENTS FOR PROGRESSIVE POSITIONS

Issue	Progressive Position	Morality	Rationale
Environmental Protection	We need more regulation.	purity	It is important that we have policies that keep our forests pristine.
Environmental Protection	We need more regulation.	authority	Regulations enable us to protect God's gift to humanity.
Environmental Protection	We need more regulation.	loyalty	We are showing insufficient loyalty to future and past generations through environmental damage.
Immigration	We should favor more immigration.	authority	Ronald Reagan: "Immigration, I believe, is one of the most important sources of America's greatness."
Immigration	We should favor more immigration.	loyalty	Immigration increases patriotism, since new arrivals are often more patriotic than others.
Immigration	We should favor more immigration.	loyalty	Companies need inexpensive labor that immigrants have always provided.
Healthcare	We should strive toward universal coverage.	purity	Universal coverage helps control diseases that might spread through the population.
Healthcare	We should strive toward universal coverage.	loyalty	Jesus said we should care for "the least of these."

Voting Access	We should fight against actions limiting the ability of citizens to vote.	loyalty	Respected American leaders have died for the right to vote. We owe it to them to make sure that everyone can do so.
Voting Access	We should fight against actions limiting the ability of citizens to vote.	purity	Full access to voting allows the purest expression of American democracy, not degraded by institutional influences.
Social Safety Net	We should invest more resources in protecting the vulnerable among us.	loyalty	The previous generation has sacrificed for us; we should support them in their final years.
Social Safety Net	We should invest more resources in protecting the vulnerable among us.	loyalty	Many of those who need help are our veterans, who have sacrificed for us.
Social Safety Net	We should invest more resources in protecting the vulnerable among us.	purity	Not investing in the safety net means our cities will become infested with filth and disease because of homelessness.

COAX METHOD 2: SHARING AN EXPERIENCE THAT ALIGNS WITH A CONSERVATIVE WORLDVIEW OR VALUE THAT SUPPORTS A PROGRESSIVE POSITION

A second way of trying to move a conservative person to empathize with your opinion is to tell them the story of a personal experience with a takeaway that supports your point of view. The hope is that by telling them a story in a way that is compelling, you activate their mirror neurons and increase the degree to which they identify with you. Your intention is that by getting them to step inside of your experience, your view of the issue becomes more than the ramblings of their political enemy. Hopefully, they will instead see your perspective as reasonable way of seeing a situation based on what you have gone through.

The worksheets that you did on lifestyle and orientation may be particularly important here, since unlike in the Agree step, you are trying to get your partner to concede that a point of view that they previously disagreed with is not completely wrong. This may be made a bit easier if you can reduce their intuitive sense of the psychological distance between you. If in the course of telling your story you can sprinkle in comments or even asides that suggest you share a conservative sensibility, your persuasive task will be helped. Even more powerfully, if you can remind the other person that you have an appreciation for conservative moral thinking, the other person is more likely to consider your conclusion as reasonable.

AN ILLUSTRATION:

You are in a conversation with a conservative about the social safety net. In the Enquire step, they told you about the neighbor of their relative who received public benefits but who they thought was more than capable of working. During the Agree step, you told them about a recent experience when you were in a dollar store where you felt judgmental of a customer in front of you who you suspected was using an EBT card to buy her groceries, but was driving a car just like yours. Your point was to convey that you sometimes think that some people receiving public benefits should not get them. Your conversation partner's body language conveyed to you that they have felt similarly judgmental about people on public assistance.

For the Coax step, you are going to tell an anecdote about your experience with your friend Steve, an Iraq war veteran who has struggled with addiction. In the setup of the story, you will discuss your lifelong friendship and how he suffered from PTSD and addiction after returning from Iraq. (You happen to mention parenthetically that you admired him for volunteering to serve; you leave out the detail that you thought the war as a horrible idea and another example of the American imperialist impulse.) The key moment of the story will be your description of the suffering Steve has experienced because of the combination of his physical and psychological problems and the severe inefficacies at the Veterans Administration. The takeaway of the story might highlight your perception that the society has been disloyal to him, and your perceptions that the insufficient level of care he gets seems foster his psychological problems to be passed down to his children.

Note that in this summary of the anecdote you might have intentionally focused not on liberal values such as caring and fairness, but instead on conservative ones such as loyalty and purity.

Anecdotes will not always be so easily modifiable in light of the moral frameworks analysis. The key point here is that in order to maximize your effectiveness, you should not only think in advance about stories in your arsenal that can be useful for various topics, but you should also re-examine whether you might learn how to tell them differently depending on whom you are trying to influence.

BROTHAMAN SEZ – SPIES LIKE US

In my workshops on white anti-racist allyship, there are usually a large portion of people who are thrown so off-center by racially problematic remarks that they have trouble making strategic conversational choices. They either become overly confrontational, or they completely disengage for fear of being disruptive—then feel guilty later for saying nothing.

In coaching them on what to do, I typically suggest that they use racist remarks as a signal that it's time to act like a spy who is behind enemy lines. Spies are not reactive; they know how to keep asking questions, and they know how to meld a sense that they are being their authentic selves along with actions purposely designed to build rapport, even with people they may detest. In the workshops, I usually think my advice about using the spy metaphor will be processed by the white anti-racists as black brilliance, but in reality, it rarely gets the intensity of head nods and compliments I think it deserves. (Sad!)

The spy attitude seems harder for white progressives to adopt than I expected. Perhaps the spy construct is deeply resonant for me because it aligns with the racism survival training that I and most black folks (and other people of color) have gotten all of our lives. Controlling our reactions in the face of disturbing behavior is something deeply ingrained in my people.

Going back generations, when unabashed racial subjugation as well as purposeful daily insults were much more common than now, black people had to learn how to hold back from expressing their own contempt and bottle up their rage, because expressing these feelings would inevitably have led led to more victimization. The same skill is relevant today; it is needed when people are questioned in settings where some white person appoints themselves as the racial privilege gatekeeper and inappropriately challenges the black person's legitimacy, whether the privilege it is about sitting in business class, cashing bank checks, or providing physician assistance to unconscious people on a plane, among other examples. Regardless of the appropriateness of expressing righteous anger at these racist challenges, the black person in these situations must calculate whether expressing their anger at the intensity they feel is only likely to make their situation worse, since the gatekeeper usually has uniformed backup.

This same ability to make good choices while upset is precisely the skill at the heart of "The Talk" that black parents have with their adolescents about surviving police encounters. To survive, people in oppressed groups have to train each other in the skill of making choices from a centered place that allows them to focus on a bigger goal in the face of deeply upsetting unfairness in the moment.

There are scars that come with a lifetime of learning that we don't really have the right to express ourselves in an unfettered manner, lest we suffer bad and sometimes fatal consequences. But it seems that with the scars come skills—namely the capacities needed to process intense feelings internally and navigate the current moment in light of a bigger objective.

Sometimes I am both amused and confused when white progressives tell a story where they talk about being overwhelmed with sadness, frustration, or rage by someone else's comments that cause them to fight or flee—knowing that neither of these leads to the changes they want to create. I find myself giving the Scooby-doo confused head tilt as I try to process the fact that they have so much trouble acting on a basic truth that is reflexive to me, and that has been known by the greatest Zen masters, my great-grandmama, and spies everywhere: no matter what people are doing to you and how you feel about it, you can access a centered place where you are able to make strategic choices about what actions you will take. Progressives who want to change the persuadable minds of those in their circles would be well served by cultivating their inner spy.

HONOR – INVITING THEM TO JOIN YOU IN THINKING BOTH OF YOU HAVE A PIECE OF THE TRUTH

The last step in the process of influencing is honoring each of your perspectives as useful within the search for truth about the topic at hand. In the Honor step, you are trying to put a bow around the conversation and make sure they don't think that they have to give up their point of view to adjust to yours. Your message is that you think that both of you have a piece of the truth, and you are inviting them to see the issue that way too.

One important psychological adjustment that is helpful to make is that you are not trying to "win" in the conversation. Your goal is not to have them bow down and say, "I now realize, oh wise and intellectually superior progressive one, that you are completely right, and I have been completely wrong." Rather, your goal is to get them to think or say something closer to, "Hmmm, I will have to think about this further." Given how staunchly many cling to their viewpoint in these divided times, creating a small crack in their protective armor is a victory.

One way to attempt to keep their defenses from snapping back into place is to explicitly remind your partner that you both experienced some level of alignment/agreement earlier. Consider saying something like, "Our exchange has felt more connected than most I have with people who sometimes see things differently. Good stuff!" You might even remind them—if it's true—that neither of your seemed to think the other person sounded crazy, like often happens in conversations.

Your task here is to help them try to hold two ideas in their minds that they may have previously thought were incompatible. Many conservatives (and not a small portion of liberals) think very categorically. Accordingly, they often support their policy preferences by adopting the view that the world is less complex than it actually is. A goal of the REACH method is to make your conversation partner comfortable with new possibilities, and the inherent uncertainty that accompanies newness. Many adherents to the REACH method have told us that in this phase of the process, it is often useful to use phrases like "I wonder whether…" or "Could it be that…" By framing the wrap-up to the conversation this way, you are reframing the disagreement and inviting them to consider that two ideas that they previously thought were unresolvable can, in fact, be resolved.

What might this look like?

ON GUN CONTROL

After you have told them about your experience where you and others felt the presence of a gun made everyone more nervous, you might say something like, "I wonder whether two things can be true: that sometimes the presence of a gun by a non-officer makes some people feel safer, and other times it makes some people feel less safe. I wonder whether it's possible that both of these things are true. What do you think?"

ON THE SOCIAL SAFETY NET

After you have told them about your lazy cousin who is working the disability system and your friend Steve the veteran, you might say something like, "Could it be that having welfare available sometimes hurts people and makes them dependent, and sometimes it helps people whose families would suffer otherwise get on their feet? If that is possible, I guess we need to think harder about which happens more, right?"

Your goal is not to get the person to concede to your superior knowledge, but rather to acknowledge that they might need to think more about the issue. Depending on each of your levels of continued interest in talking about the topic, you might agree to get more information and think about topic more deeply.

KNOW WHEN TO WALK AWAY, KNOW WHEN TO RUN

It is important to make good choices about when to close the conversation. If your engagement of the person by the REACH method has been successful, you may have shaken a belief they deeply held. This can be disturbing, especially to someone highly oriented toward order and stability. If you have created a moment of pause in them with both of you feeling connected to each other, the best move may be to transition away from that topic. If you stay on the topic too long, sometimes people will want to reflexively revert back to the certainty of their original belief, thus undoing the good work you have done. It very well may be that your best move is to leave the conversation with no definitive conclusion except that more needs to be known and thought about. Conversely, sometimes lingering in the conversation might create an epiphany for your conversation partner. You will have to let your sense of discernment guide you.

My hope is that you spend some time actually trying to work on your ability to engage with the REACH method. To progress toward mastery, you should make conscious choices about the level of challenge you take on as you work the method. Here are four different degrees of challenge:

LEVEL 1

Engage a fellow progressive friend whom you enlist to help you practice. You can work together to find an issue that you disagree about or at least that you support or oppose at significantly different levels. One advantage of engaging a friend who knows you are practicing is that you can get direct feedback on issues like: Did you make them feel heard in the Enquire phase? How sincerely did they feel your attempt to Agree with them? How coherent or compelling were you when you tried to Coax them to your position? Did your attempt to Honor them resonate?

LEVEL 2

Engage a fellow progressive on a topic that you disagree with while using the method unbeknownst to them. If you find that you need to explain why you are pursuing a conversation, you might tell them that you are joining an effort to make sure progressives retain the ability to have good dialogue so as to avoid fractures in the movement.

LEVEL 3

If you have a conservative friend with whom you have a strong connection, you might explain that you are working on your dialogue skills. Depending on the person and your relationship, you might be able to get direct feedback on your performance, as in Level 1.

LEVEL 4

Engaging actual conservatives who don't know you are working a method is what your ultimate goal as you achieve mastery of this method. When you are first engaging at this level, it is wise to choose topics, people, and settings with great discernment so that you maximize your chance that the experience is a success.

QUESTIONS TO ASK BEFORE PRACTICING THE COAX AND HONOR STEPS

1. What are the issues I am not overly triggered by that might be good fodder for practicing these steps?

2. Who are people with whom I can have a conversation that are not likely to upset me and throw me off center?

3. Whom do I trust to give me good feedback on my performance in engaging the steps?

QUESTIONS TO ASK AFTER PRACTICING THE COAX AND HONOR STEPS

1. How did the relaxation methods and listening tips work?

2. What was the effect of the Enquire step on you? What do you think was the effect on your conversation partner?

3. How successful were you at adding atmospheric elements to the Agree and Coax steps? Were there elements that felt smoother coming out of your mouth than others?

4. How did you feel about how well you executed the Coax step? What was your perception of your conversation partner's reactions to how you engaged?

5. What was the overall impact of the process on you? Do you want to keep trying this? Why or why not?

QUESTIONS FOR GROUP DISCUSSION

1. Has this process had any impact on: how we communicate with non-conservatives? Our feelings about conservatives? Our insight about ourselves?

2. What is the impact of engaging in this way on my desire to be a progressive change agent? To what extent is this a useful way of trying to advance the progressive cause?

3. This process has been pitched as having a spiritual dimension. To what extent is that actually the case for each of us?

4. What is the impact of engaging this way on our level of hopefulness for American democracy?

5. What are smart and less smart ways of talking about what we are learning to other progressives?

CHAPTER 8

CONCLUSION:
MOBILIZING COMPASSIONATE DIALOGUE IN OUR HYPER-DIVIDED TIME

This handbook is written as guidance to a progressive movement which has understandable opposition to President Trump's impact on politics but that is paradoxically aping the qualities in him that progressives detest. Too often, we progressives interact with conservative people in a way that is condescending, dismissive, and fundamentally disrespectful. This is what President Trump does to us, and progressives, especially white ones, are doing this on a massive scale with conservatives they work with, live next to, pray with, and love. Not only is this spiritually regressive, but such behavior is also politically self-defeating.

Jerkish behavior by Trump and his supporters is what progressives hate and what Trump supporters often find energizing. When progressives return it, this fits the Trump supporters' sense of grievance and resentment. And this response only makes support for him grow stronger. The ironies of this situation are many.

Even though Trump's negative behavior is a contagion affecting the entire culture, the problematic behavior of white progressives merits special attention. It is the white population that is deeply divided on its support for Trump. To remind you of 2016 election results, here are the portions of Trump support by the four biggest racial groups:

Support for Donald Trump in 2016, by race
- Black 8%
- Latino 27%
- Asian 28%
- White 58%

It is white progressives who have the most access to Trump supporters in their circle of contact—their families, their friends, their acquaintances, their fellow worshipers, and their neighbors. It is the white progressive population that has the best potential for weakening support for Trump if they reduce their unhelpful behavior towards Trump supporters. Modern America is still deeply physically and socially segregated. Even though many white progressives have created liberal bubbles for themselves, it remains the case that white progressives are much more likely to have Trump supporters and conservatives within their circles of contact, influence and intimacy.

Undoubtedly, the vast majority of Trump supporters cannot be moved from their points of view. Political experts vary in the estimate of how many Trump supporters should be considered persuadable, but estimates usually vary from 8 to 20 percent. If it is possible to change the minds of persuadable Trump voters, it is generally going to be on white progressives whom this will fall, because it is white progressives who have regular social contact with them. But too many of you get frustrated or angry, avoid talking about politics if disagreement emerges, or become so noxious as to eliminate any possibility of changing their minds.

My hope is that you not only take on the idea of engaging conservatives as part of your duty as a progressive, but also that you begin talking to other progressives about engaging conservatives as an imperative within the progressive movement. This should not be the only thing that progressives do, of course. But it is a task that should not be neglected.

One way of thinking about this is to look at this handbook as attempting to bring what is sometimes called "deep canvassing" to a broader scale. Deep canvassing is an approach to mobilizing election volunteers that is very different from traditional canvassing, wherein volunteers or paid workers create encounters with potential voters (typically at their front door) and the objective of the canvasser to is to deliver information from a standard script in about 1-3 minutes. In contrast, deep canvassing is focused on potentially changing people's minds by listening deeply to them, empathizing with their point of view and the experience related to it, and gently trying to revisit their voting behavior in light of new concerns. In a deep canvassing effort, managers of poll workers have come to regard 10 minutes per encounter as appropriate.

This handbook could be can regarded as an attempt to extend the reach of deep canvassing. In addition to the progressive community raising money for thousands of deep canvassers to be deployed to select areas, the aspiration here is to catalyze deep canvassing on a much larger scale. There will only be so much money that will ever be available to deep canvassing efforts; at best such efforts are never likely to involve more tens of thousands of deep canvassers. My aspiration is to foster a cultural shift among progressives so that millions of progressives are using deep canvassing methods with people in their circles of contact.

Using the REACH method is electoral strategy and it is a method every American can learn as an act of patriotism and national self-protection. As I discussed in Chapter 1, tensions along ideological lines are something that Vladimir Putin is fostering on purpose. He is mobilizing hundreds of millions of dollars to engage social media specialists to fill up Americans' social media with content designed to make us disdain each other and make it more difficult for Americans to talk to each other with mutual respect.

This handbook has instructed progressives to train themselves toward better behavior, and exhorted them to talk about this with other liberals. In addition, progressives need to be talking to their conservative friends and family members about the fact that America is under an attack aimed at dividing it. We should make the case that the disdain that progressives and conservatives frequently show to each other is not only at odds with the spirit of exchange in a healthy democracy, but that these unhelpful ways are being encouraged by America's enemies.

There is one more reason besides boosting the progressive movement and helping democracy overall that explains my sincere hope that you make these methods part of your regular life. Most progressives have a core presumption that operating from our highest self means coming from a place of compassion and empathy, and that this is psychologically and spiritually healthier for us. Coming at someone from a place of condescension and superiority may indeed feel better in the short run, especially if that person is acting on these same lower impulses. My experience though is that when people train themselves to transform their contempt into compassion, they notice that they feel better about themselves after interactions, even if they do not change anyone's mind.

If someone is even vaguely connected to a spiritual tradition, operating from a place of empathy and compassion tends to help people feel like they are enacting their faith. And even if a spiritual practice is not a part of their lives, most people just feel better knowing that they made choices to try to increase the amount of compassion in the world, instead of doing the opposite. No matter whether we have a spiritual practice or not, a general truth is that contempt breeds contempt, and compassion creates compassion.

WE NEED MORE DIALOGUE ABOUT DIALOGUE

My hope is that the next time you are in a conversation about divides in the American body politic, you will talk honestly about the way the contempt and divisions are fomented by Americans' enemies. You should talk about the idea that Americans should unite around listening to each other and that we should try to extend some basic human grace even to those with whom we vehemently disagree. And importantly, you should talk about how difficult it is for you to do what you know, in your best moments, you need to do.

My hope is that the next time you are in a conversation with other progressives about those awful closed-minded Trump supporters, you remind them that no one ever changed their mind because a condescending peer shamed them into it. If you are part of a faith community, my hope is that the next time the issue of practicing your faith comes up, you make the point that talking compassionately to conservatives is part of your spiritual practice and potentially can be part of theirs too. Talking about how hard it can be for you to resist the impulse to look down on conservatives will make this conversation more honest and effective.

There is much on the line as the 2020 election proceeds. With some justification, progressive people see the prospect of the reelection of Donald Trump as much more dire than merely four more years of an administration that will roll back policy gains won over the decades. Liberals see his reelection as bringing about an even more fundamental degradation of institutions and practices that are the core what America is. Of course, Trump supporters feel similarly, although they have a rather different definition of the "America" that is at risk of being lost if Trump loses. No matter what happens, half of the nation will be bitterly disappointed, and that half will tell themselves that the election represents a fundamental turning point in the decline of the country.

Of course, some of this may be exaggerated. But what I think should not be underestimated is the damage that will come to our democracy if Americans on opposite sides of the ideological divide continue to regard each other and talk to each other as enemies; we must move our culture to look at ideological opponents as comrades who have similar goals but different ways of going about them. If we continue to lose our ability to embody curiosity, compassion, and basic respect, the erosion of the sense of national unity that has been important to Americans will be something that both conservatives and progressives will admit has been lost.

And let us also remember that no matter who wins, the period after the most divisive election in many decades will need to be a time of healing. The conservative movement is not likely to produce people interested in this, whether conservatives win or lose. It will be up to progressives to do this healing work. So we might as well start now, thus increasing the chance the progressives won't be the ones who need to be consoled.

After the Constitutional Convention, someone asked Ben Franklin what kind of system the participants had handed to the citizens. His answer was, "A republic, if you can keep it."

Nothing less than that is at stake regarding how Americans engage each other about politics. My fervent hope is that white progressives will step forward in this critical moment and do what they should to protect the country.

APPENDIX 1:
RESOURCES ON EMPATHY BASED ENGAGEMENT

The following are some resources that might be helpful for progressives who want to further explore empathy-based approaches to engaging across the political divide.

Better Angels is a national citizens' movement to reduce political polarization in the United States by bringing liberals and conservatives together to understand each other.

Knock Every Door is an organization that is dedicated to deep canvassing for liberal causes. The organization recruits and trains volunteers to go out into communities across the country to start conversations about the progressive change our country needs.

Listen First Coalition is an umbrella organizing group that supports many organizations dedicated to compassionate listening and empathy-based interactions. Its goal is to do organizing events, train leaders, and support collaborations that will grow the movement for better and more dialogue across differences.

Living Room Conversations is an on-line resource that produces a conversational model developed by dialogue experts in order to facilitate connection between across lines of difference. The resource currently has 100 conversation guides on many topics.

National Coalition for Dialogue & Deliberation (NCDD) is a network of people (many are professional facilitators) focused on bringing people together across divides to discuss, decide, and take action together effectively on difficult issues.

SMART Politics is an 8,000 person Facebook group focused on helping progressives conduct more effective social media interactions with conservatives.

Working America is the political organizing arm of the AFL-CIO; membership is made up of non-union individuals. The organization uses deep canvassing approaches extensively to advocate for progressive causes and candidates.

APPENDIX 2:
A TOOL TO IMPROVE CONVERSATIONS ABOUT PRESIDENT TRUMP

What should do if you find yourself headed toward a conversation about people's opinions of President Trump?

In this handbook, I have suggested that the way to connect with and maybe influence people is to shift the focus to values or experiences instead of simply belief, opinions, and the "facts" that support them. This is hard to do – maybe impossible to do—when the topic is the binary choice that elections represent. But there is something you can do to make these moments a bit less divisive. The core strategy is to begin the conversation by offering a few sincere compliments about President Trump, and to ask your conversation partner for some critiques of him.

Here is how you might do this:

1. Mention your concern that a Like/Dislike conversation about Trump may be difficult.

2. Tell your conversation partners that in order to shift the energy of the exchange, you want to suggest something unconventional. Say that you want to perform a verbal gift exchange consisting of comments about the President.

3. Tell them you are going to give them X number of compliments about President Trump. Tell them that after that, you will ask them to offer to you X-1 critiques of him. Tell them that experts have found that this preliminary exchange is a good for shifting the energy in a conversation between Trump supporters and Trump opponents.

4. Offer him as many compliments as you can say in a way that is not snarky, backhanded, or implying a criticism. (It may be useful to practice this in the mirror or with another progressive).

5. After you offer your X number of compliments, invite them to offer X – 1 critiques. If they offer specific actions (e.g. "He did not rescind DACA," or "He did not recind Obamacare") clarify that you were hoping they would offer compliments to his character, not specific actions.

6. After the person tells you his critiques, say something like: "Thanks for doing that. I think we will have a better conversation about the good and bad of President Trump because we have reminded ourselves that he is neither all good nor all bad."

To assist you, here are twelve compliments for you to pull from:

1. Compared to many presidents, he is entertaining, and often funny. (Note: you don't have to like his sense of humor to admit he is funnier than G.H.W. Bush or Jimmy Carter).

2. He is persuasive (even if not to you).

3. He appears to love his family (Extra comments about his odd affection for Ivanka are not helpful when making this point).

4. He has a strong personality that many others like to follow.

5. He is now and has always been good at self-promotion.

6. He has authentic passion for some problems.

7. He gives voice to a sense of grievance for tens of millions that America. Working through this grievance is important for the country. (You don't have to think these grievances are valid to acknowledge this).

8. He can simplify problems in ways that are engaging to a big portion of the population.

9. He is now and has always been good at influencing the media.

10. He is relentless in pursuit of things he wants.

11. He is effective in mobilizing his political allies.

12. He exudes confidence, which inspires many people.

Feel free to add other compliments; if possible, the compliments should be qualities, not specific accomplishments.

The key for this method to work is that you appear sincere in the compliment. You need to be able to give the compliment without talking about the downsides of this quality, or adding a criticism or something sarcastic.

When you execute this method, you are trying to model for your conversation partner that there is a way to transcend the "all or nothing" thinking that tends to undermine conversations about President Trump and exchanges across the divide generally. This will not only improve the energy between you, but getting them to remind themselves of their critiques of the president may give you something to build on that you can use later in the conversation.

APPENDIX 3:
CONSERVATIVE VERSUS LIBERAL LIFESTYLE ASSESSMENT

Below is a self-assessment tool that invites you explore reflect on some characteristics you have in relationship to one or two conservatives you know reasonably well. This exercise is particularly valuable if you are working in a group, because you can see larger patterns of personal differences that may influence your thinking about the implications of the ideological divide.

Step 1: Put your first initial on where you are on each of these scales. **Be honest!**

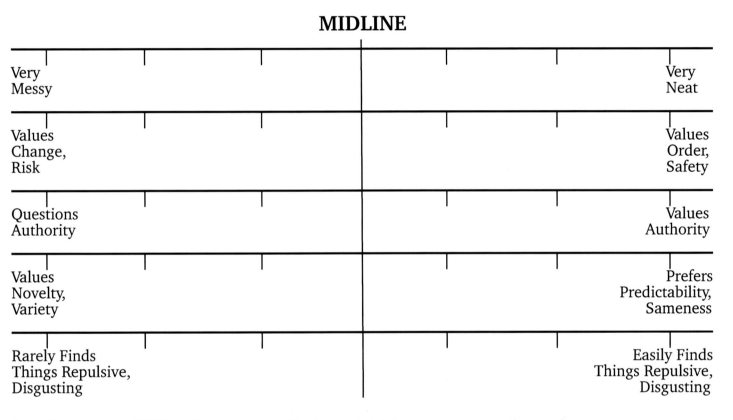

MIDLINE

Very Messy						Very Neat
Values Change, Risk						Values Order, Safety
Questions Authority						Values Authority
Values Novelty, Variety						Prefers Predictability, Sameness
Rarely Finds Things Repulsive, Disgusting						Easily Finds Things Repulsive, Disgusting

Step 2: Draw a solid line that connects all of your initials, so you can easily see the pattern.

Step 3: Do Step 1 again, this time assessing a conservative person whom you know well. Let's call that person Conservative #1. Assess them using the scale above. When you are done, use a dotted to connect the initials of Conservative #1 down the sheet. Count the number of dimensions where Conservative #1 scored to the right of you. _____

Step 4: If you know another conservative person reasonably well (Conservative #2), do the same process, connecting that person's initials with a double dotted line. Count the number of times Conservative #2 scored to the right of you. _____

Step 5: Reflect on the significance of the results. For a large number of progressives who do this exercise, the conservatives they know are to the right of them on 4 or 5 of these dimensions. Such a finding tends to confirm the idea that conservatism and liberalism are not merely political preferences but also embody an orientation around many lifestyle choices that have little to do with politics.

Step 6: If you are in a group: Take note of what portion of the conservatives that were assessed had four or five answers that were to the right of the progressive survey taker. Have a conversation about the implications of this finding for your understanding of conservatism and liberalism.

APPENDIX 4:
AGENDA TEMPLATE FOR GROUP MEETINGS

To progress through all of the phases of the REACH method, a group should plan on meeting 4-7 times. It is reasonable to combine the Reflect and Enquire methods in one meeting, and to combine the Coax and Honor phases in one meeting.

It is useful to create the expectation that every person conveys how much or how little they engaged the methods since the last meeting. This practice makes the meetings an accountability check.

Meetings should be planned for between 45 and 120 minutes, not including any time for eating.

Check-In

Is there anything that has happened since we last met that has significantly affected your ability to engage the material or to stay focused this session? *(This gives people a chance to talk about illnesses, death, or other life events that might be on their heart or mind.)*

Triumphs and Trials

Apart from what you intended to do with respect to the homework, did you have any encounters across the divide that were chances to practice any phases of the REACH method?

Discussion of Reflections on Engaging the Homework

- What level of difficulty did you intend to engage?

- What actually happened when you tried the methods?

- What are the lessons you learned?

- What are the collective lessons?

Review of Next Phase of the REACH Method

- What are the key things to remember to assure success in executing this phase of the method?

Working on the Skill We Discussed Today

- What are useful people, topics, and settings for each of you to engage the methods?

- What do you think will be the biggest obstacles that might keep you from you successfully engaging these methods?

- What level of difficulty do you plan to engage with the methods?

Made in the USA
Monee, IL
08 June 2024

59499264R00062